BAD BLOOD

The Families Who Made the West Wild

ROBERT BARR SMITH

TWODOT®

GUILFORD, CONNECTICUT
HELENA, MONTANA

AN IMPRINT OF ROWMAN & LITTLEFIELD

A · TWODOT® · BOOK

An imprint of Rowman & Littlefield

Distributed by NATIONAL BOOK NETWORK

Copyright © 2014 by Robert Barr Smith

TwoDot is a registered trademark of Rowman & Littlefield.

British Library Cataloguing-in-Publication Information is available on file.

Library of Congress Cataloging-in-Publication Data is available on file.

ISBN 978-1-4930-0613-7

∞™ The paper used in this publication meets the minimum requirements of American National Standard for Information Sciences—Permanence of Paper for Printed Library Materials, ANSI/NISO Z39.48-1992.

CONTENTS

Foreword v

Chapter 1—"We'll wait.": The Dalton Boys at Coffeyville. 1
Chapter 2—Empty Men: The Fleagles. 11
Chapter 3—Two Banks at Once: Disaster at Northfield. 19
Chapter 4—Massacre in Greene County: The Youngs. 26
Chapter 5—Debacle on the Border:
    The Christian Boys Panic at Nogales 35
Chapter 6—Vicious and Inept:
    The DeAutremonts and the Railroad 51
Chapter 7—The Wrong Town: The McCarty Clan at Delta 59
Chapter 8—Pioneers: The Reno Boys
    and the Sport of Train Robbery. 74
Chapter 9—Like Father, Like Son: The Clements Family. 78
Chapter 10—Mama's Boys: The Barker Gang and Friends 85
Chapter 11—Bad to the Bone: The Selman Brothers 95
Chapter 12—England's Rejects: Ben and Billy Thompson. . . . 102
Chapter 13—A Vanished Yesterday: The Sutton-Taylor Feud . . 109
Chapter 14—Just Plain Nasty: The Casey Boys 116
Chapter 15—The Plague of Cochise County:
    The Clanton Clan 121
Chapter 16—Two-Bit Tough Guys: The Martins 130
Chapter 17—The Kansas Horror: The Bloody Benders 140
Chapter 18—The Bumbling Lawyers:
    Jennings & Jennings, Esq. 152

CONTENTS

Chapter 19—Dirty Gold: The Reynolds Brothers 165

Chapter 20—Revenge: The McCluskies 173

Chapter 21—Late Beginners: Rube and Jim Burrow 182

Chapter 22—Just Down-Home Folks: The Newton Boys 187

Chapter 23—A Flash in the Pan: The Poe-Hart Gang 194

Chapter 24—The Scourge of the Railroad: The Sontags 203

Chapter 25—A Rich Assortment of Trash:
        Some Lesser Scum 209

Epilogue 216

Bibliography 218

Index 223

About the Author 230

Foreword

The Old West abounded with outlaws, bandits, killers, rustlers, rapists, assorted trash of all kinds. So did the wild days of the early twentieth century. A great many of these hoodlums were career criminals; hurting other people in various ways was what they did for a living and, sometimes, just for fun. The way they saw the world, the outlawing business beat the hell out of following a mule's behind all day or pushing contrary cows who didn't want to go where you wanted them to.

To folks who shared this flawed perspective, honest work was somehow belittling and certainly nothing out of the ordinary that a man could brag about. Besides, many of them seemed to think that riding on the wrong side of the law somehow "made them somebody." Robin Hood and Dick Turpin were long dead, but in the eyes of a lot of young punks at least they could be successors to some famous outlaws of yesteryear. It is highly unlikely most of them had ever heard of Robin or Dick, but they could find role models from their own time easily enough.

It somehow helped to make you somebody if you gave yourself a "brag name," especially since most of the young hoodlums who took one were no smarter than the average cow, and some were clearly mentally vacant, which was often a great help to the law. Take for example an Oklahoma loser called Bob Rogers, who, when faced by a large posse, demanded to know whether they had a warrant for him.

Now, he'd just finished killing one lawman and wounding another, so he should not have been surprised by the terse answer of the deputy US marshal in charge: "No; we don't need one." Whereupon Rogers jerked up the muzzle of his rifle toward the officers, prompting seven or eight possemen together to terminally ventilate him. *Sic semper stupid.*

The history of western crime is full of swashbuckling names, such as the Verdigris Kid, the Narrow-Gauge Kid, Billy the Kid, and the Polkadot Kid (just a few of the punks who called themselves "kid" something or other). Add to these Black-Faced Charlie, Rustling Bob, Little Bill, Red Buck, Texas Jack, Chicken Lucas, Black Jack (at least two of those), Dynamite Dick, Flyspeck Billy (his leader was called Lame Johnny), Rattlesnake Jake, and on and on.

Later on would come Pretty Boy, Machinegun Jack, Skeet, Big Bob, Killer (several of those), Two Gun, Shotgun, Mad Dog, Chaw Jimmie, The Owl, and Boobie Clark, whose *nom de crime* pretty well describes the intellectual level of the average professional criminal.

A good many of the hoodlums with self-christened snappy names turned out to be heap big smoke and no fire. They quickly discovered that all was not as it was painted in the tabloids and penny-dreadful paperbacks: The living was very hard on the run, and the lawmen of the day (including their posses) were very tough cobs who did not give up easily, especially if the reward was sizable.

And so, like criminals of a later day, the punks of yesteryear generally died young and violently, either full of bullets or on the end of a rope, and very few learned anything. Those who lived were likely to spend their salad days watching the world go by through a set of iron bars.

There was precious little nobility about most of them. During the gang years, quite a number rolled over on their comrades, testifying either gladly or at least enthusiastically against their fellow knights of the road. If they were promised immunity from the noose and maybe a reduction in sentence, loyalty to their friends and accomplices magically faded away to insignificance.

There was one thing many of them had in common: Most of them were farm boys who shared a common goal, pretty accurately expressed by one of the Newton brothers: "I wanted something . . . and I knew I would never get it following a mule's ass and dragging cotton sacks down them middles."

You could say something good about some of them, if you tried hard enough. Most of them loved their mothers, and a few even visited home from time to time, like the Dalton boys. A few were good family men, like Bill Doolin, at least as often as crime and flight would permit a visit to the family. Some liked dogs or horses; a few even went to church sometimes.

But by and large they were, as Long John Silver would say, a scurvy lot.

The leading candidate for scumbag-in-chief would have to be David Rudabaugh, better known to all and sundry as Dirty Dave. Besides his foul and violent personality, Dave was famous for his penetrating odor, a stench that preceded his arrival by a quarter of an hour.

Dave dabbled in robbery early on, fumbled his way into the hands of the law, testified against his former friends, and then blew town for safer climes. Those climes included Las Vegas, New Mexico, where he became a part of the criminal band led by HooDoo Brown, the town justice of the peace. He spent a little time running with Billy the Kid, too, and at last turned up around Tombstone as part of the so-called "Cowboy faction."

When Dave ran out of welcome, as he inevitably did, he went off to Mexico. There he inflicted himself on the small Chihuahua town of Parral, where, as usual, he quickly became a major irritant to the population—but not so much for his penetrating odor as for his anger. He became upset during a card game—apparently he wasn't winning—and ended up killing a couple of the locals. They responded by

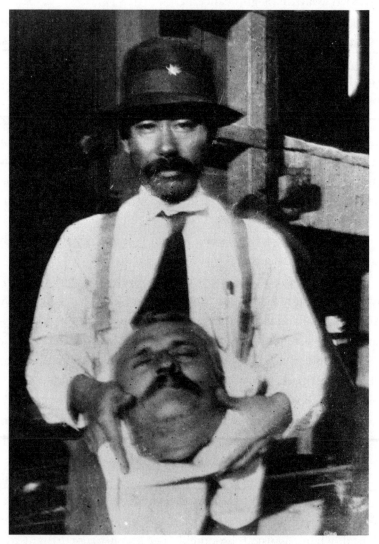

Dirty Dave Rudabaugh's head WESTERN HISTORY COLLECTIONS, UNIVERSITY
OF OKLAHOMA LIBRARY

permanently removing his head, impaling it on a stake, and parading it around the town, hat, mangy mustache and all. It became the centerpiece of a sort of ad hoc fiesta.

Whatever happened to the various pieces of Dave, nobody noticeably missed the whole man. And so it was with most of the rest of the outlaws: They not only were generally worthless and dim-witted, but also seldom mourned when a bullet or a noose finally got them.

A good many of them, though, varied the pattern somewhat by being related and running together. The *Muskogee Phoenix* newspaper told the tale of the Davis family, whose two sons were in the Fort Smith jail awaiting shipment to the penitentiary. The boys' mother and sister traveled to Fort Smith to say good-bye. They were astonished—and presumably distressed—to find that husband and father Davis had gotten there before them, been arrested, and was lodged in the same jail as his sons.

Frequently, family members were in the pen together, and back on the owlhoot trail when they got out, having learned absolutely nothing. The relations in the stories in this book are not only brothers and fathers and sons, but a variety of in-laws, an uncle, and even a couple of mothers. All of them share something, however.

Bad blood.

CHAPTER 1

"We'll wait."

The Dalton Boys at Coffeyville

Coffeyville, Kansas, was a sleepy, peaceful town, a civilized place where the citizens spent their days engaged in honest toil and otherwise were concerned with family, school, church, and a multitude of lodges and associations. Nobody in town carried a gun, and that included the town marshal, whose business was in fact working as a school principal. Most people used a buggy or wagon to get about their daily chores; saddle horses were not often seen.

And so it was that the citizens of little Coffeyville were not prepared for what came to them and their town on a clear, fine morning in October of 1892. The trouble began when five dusty young men rode into town and dismounted near the busy square on which the town's two banks fronted. The Condon and the First National, both open for business, shared the square with a number of other businesses, including two hardware stores.

The dusty young men were unexceptional, but even so they stuck out, as the expression went, "like a sore thumb." For one thing, all were mounted on good horses, and for emphasis, all wore long dusters and all were well armed with both rifles and handguns. To top it off, these strangers were well known to a good many people in and around the town, for they and their family had lived close to Coffeyville for several years.

Now consider: With a lot of little towns with banks to choose from, why pick the one town where you are eminently recognizable? The answer seems to be twofold: First, the typical young western criminal was arrogant; second, little Coffeyville had *two* banks. And thereby hangs a tale.

These intruders were the famous Dalton gang, Bob, Gratton, and young Emmett. With them rode two other professional thugs: Dick Broadwell and Bill Powers. The Daltons were already veterans of several more-or-less successful robberies down in Oklahoma, and during the last one they had pointlessly shot down two innocent, unarmed bystanders, one of whom died of his wounds. Both of the victims were doctors, who along with clergymen were a protected species in the West. Now every man's hand was against the gang.

So the sensible decision was made to vamoose. That they intended to do, once they attended to those two banks. First, however, they needed a stake to go far away and live high on the hog. Second, there was a record to be set.

The Dalton boys were cousins to the Younger brothers, then cooling their heels in a Minnesota prison after their disastrous attempt to rob a bank up in Northfield, Minnesota. Even the long-lived James-Younger gang had never been part of a two-bank raid, and so Bob Dalton wanted to do what even that famous outlaw aggregation had never done, and he said so.

Now Bob, although he was the leader of the pack, was not eldest of the boys. That was brother Gratton, but handsome Bob at least knew enough to come in out of the rain. Gratton—generally called

Grat—didn't. He was dumber than a rock, as the kids say, interested primarily in booze, cards, and beating up other people, and that was on his good days. Emmett was only eighteen, and strictly a follower.

Adeline Dalton, mother to these three, was a good woman, in spite of being a Younger. She had married very young, and husband Lewis Dalton, considerably older than she, had done little but follow the horses here and there, as tout, betting man, and so on. But he did get home often enough that poor Adeline had fifteen kids.

Because of Adeline's heroic efforts, largely single-handed, all the youngsters turned out to be law-abiding, useful citizens, except for Bob, Grat, Emmett, and Bill. Now the first three sons were about to break her heart.

Bob thought he had the mechanics of the raid all figured out, but he had made two colossal mistakes in planning: He chose the wrong town to invade and did no reconnaissance worthy of the name. He and his band of boobies simply camped the night before along a stream called Onion Creek and then rode casually into town the next morning.

There they discovered the first flaw in Bob's battle plan: Things were not as they used to be. The city fathers, in the name of civic improvement, had removed a very important detail. And since there had been no recon done, the gang didn't know things had changed in Coffeyville since they last saw the little town.

For when the Daltons approached the site of the hitching rack most convenient to the banks, they found it gone. "Well, I'll be damned," quoth Bob the great leader, "they've taken down the rack," or something like that, stating the obvious. So the gang settled for an alley, where they tied their all-important horses to a pipe behind the police judge's house. It was farther from the banks, but the boys didn't seem to care. They were the Dalton gang, after all.

They pulled their rifles from the saddle boots and sauntered across the square. A storekeeper sweeping the walk in front of his business immediately spotted and recognized them, and the word quickly spread around the square—the Dalton boys are in town! There couldn't be much doubt what they were there for. In any case, the sight of five dusty young men carrying rifles and riding good horses was enough to pique the curiosity of most westerners, especially in a peaceful town.

Now, although none of the townsmen carried a gun, the two hardware stores fronting on the square had an ample stock. In short order, they were handing out rifles and ammunition to anybody who wanted arms. There were plenty of takers.

Bob and Emmett barged into the First National, while Grat led Powers and Broadwell to rob the Condon. Both parties turned their rifles on the bank personnel. Give us the money, they commanded. So far, so good . . . at least at the First National. There the bankers began to gather money, although they were as slow in doing it as they dared to be.

Over at the Condon, it was a different story. There Grat was in charge—sort of—and promptly demonstrated the paucity of his intellect. First he collected a monstrous sack of coins, an estimated two hundred pounds of them. It is not recorded just how he thought to move this unwieldy burden to a horse, their mounts being parked some distance away in the alley, much less mount an escape carrying this massive burden.

In any event, Grat now turned his attention to the vault, where the real money would be. Open the vault said he, and gutsy young teller Charlie Ball looked Grat right in the eye and told the lie of his life. "I can't open it," he said innocently. "The time lock is still set." Another bank employee helpfully rattled the handle on the vault. He was careful not to pull, of course, because the vault door would have swung open.

It was the middle of the morning on a business day, and the streets were busy. The idea that the vault was still locked at such a time was preposterous, but Grat bought it.

"When does it open?" he asked.

Oct. 5ᵗʰ 1892 ~

Condon Bank WESTERN HISTORY COLLECTIONS, UNIVERSITY OF OKLAHOMA LIBRARY

Ball quickly thought up a time ten minutes or so away, and Grat's response sealed the fate of the gang with one of the truly classic responses in outlaw history.

"We'll wait."

And wait they did, long enough for the townsmen to arm themselves and get into position. As a newspaper article later noted, "eight minutes was the time consumed by Cashier Ball in his one-act skit of 'the Bogus Time Lock.'" It was time enough.

And so, about when Grat began to wonder if he was being flimflammed, Bob and Emmett came out of the First National with a bag of money, somebody took a shot at them, and the fat was in the fire. The first of some two hundred bullets and shot slammed into the Condon at the same time, and Broadwell took a round in the arm, crippling his ability to shoot back. It soon dawned on even Grat that it was high time to get out of there.

Now he could have led the way out a side door, putting the bank walls between him and those deadly rifles at the hardware stores. He had to know there was another exit; in fact, a bank customer had entered that way during the holdup, abruptly retreating when he saw all those guns.

But Grat and his men went out the front door instead, running right through the wide-open killing zone in the square before the bank. Bullets slammed into them as they sprinted desperately for their horses, now so very, very far away, puffs of dust jetting from their clothing as the slugs struck.

Grat, already wounded, got a fatal bullet into the temporary town marshal, who in the confusion appeared with his back to Grat. But Grat quickly was down and dying in the alley, hit by a bullet from the rifle of livery stable owner John Kloehr and maybe others as well. Powers was also dead in that grubby alley. Broadwell was mortally wounded but managed to mount and ride half a mile or so until he pitched off his horse and landed dead as a doornail.

Meanwhile, Bob and Emmett had sensibly run back inside the First National and right on out the back door. Bob killed a young clerk in the street behind the bank, and then he and Emmett circled up behind the square. There Bob shot down two more citizens in a cross street; they too were looking away, toward the square and the front of the bank Bob and Emmett had just left.

Still another man had been hit in the chest inside one of the hardware stores, but he was carrying a heavy iron spanner in his pocket, and the bullet struck the spanner. That citizen got nothing but a monstrous bruise and a good story. One of the bankers had been shot through the mouth, but he would defy the odds and live on.

By the time Bob and Emmett reached their horses, they were in plain view from the square. Before they could mount, they had to face a torrent of fire from the town defenders. Bob went down with a wound from a rifle round. He was lying in the dirt still working his rifle and hitting nothing until he took another bullet from deadly John Kloehr, reputed to the best shot in Coffeyville. Emmett managed to get on his horse, still carrying the feed sack of loot, but with more courage than sense he turned back, reaching down for his dead or dying brother.

There's some mythology about what Bob said to Emmett, a last heroic "die game" or something like that. The chances are that Bob was either already dead or too far gone to say anything at all, but it makes a good story. And then Emmett, already nailed with several rifle bullets, took both barrels from the shotgun of Carey Seaman, the town barber. The rounds blew him out of the saddle, and the battle of Coffeyville was over.

Emmett was miraculously still alive. He was quickly moved to the upstairs office of Dr. Wells, who set about trying to save Emmett's life. While the doctor was working on Emmett, a party of townsmen appeared, equipped with malicious intent and a length of rope. Their plan was simple: Attach one end to Emmett's neck and the other to a

Dead Daltons WESTERN HISTORY COLLECTIONS, UNIVERSITY OF OKLAHOMA LIBRARY

convenient pole outside the doctor's window. Emmett would then be flung out the window without benefit of clergy.

The doctor, true to the Hippocratic oath, dissented from that sensible notion, finally saying to the would-be executioners, "Why bother? This man is going to die anyway."

"Are you sure, Doc?"

"Hell, yes," said the redoubtable physician. "Did you ever hear of a patient of mine getting well?"

That broke the climate of anger, somebody laughed, and Emmett would live to face long years in a Kansas prison.

Brother Bill Dalton now got into the act, coming to Coffeyville with the long-suffering Adeline. He succeeded in making an insulting ass of himself, apparently his normal pompous manner. Bill later turned outlaw—not very successfully—and managed to get himself killed down in Oklahoma after an amateurish robbery in Longview, Texas. So poor Adeline had still another sorrow to bear.

All Grat, Bob, Powers, and Broadwell got was a hole in the ground, instead of the outlaw record they coveted. There was no tombstone, either. All the monument accorded them was a piece of ordinary pipe . . . the same pipe to which they had tied their horses in that deadly alley.

The Coffeyville saga did not end there. It took on a life of its own, particularly with regard to the legend of "The Sixth Rider." The burning issue raised by this legend is simply whether there was one more outlaw along on the raid, and if so, who he was, or even she. Thousands of words have been spent on the question with no sure result.

The most talked-about candidate for sixth robber is Bill Doolin, longtime professional outlaw and erstwhile Dalton gang member. His tale is that he was invited along on the raid but did not get to the main event because his horse went lame, and the fight was over before he could steal another one. Once the fight was over, Doolin and his new mount galloped south toward Oklahoma, starting, according to deathless legend,

> . . . a ride that has ever since been the admiration
> of horsemen in the Southwest . . . Doolin . . . crossed
> the Territory like a flying wraith, a ghostly rider
> saddled upon the wind.

Until he rejoined the remnants of the old gang down in Indian Territory, a very long distance indeed, even for a flying wraith.

Some horse. Some story.

Then there is the storybook tale of Julia Johnson, the love of Emmett's life, who faithfully waited for him all through the prison years. No she didn't. They did marry, but it is clear that he never laid eyes on her until after he had finished his sentence after Coffeyville, and she had married at least once while Emmett was in jail.

But pleasant legends die hard, mostly because nobody wants to be the executioner. Julia also has been nominated as the Sixth Rider, a notion about as fanciful as the "ghostly rider saddled upon the wind." Since at the time she didn't know Emmett from Adam's off ox, she is unlikely to have gone a-robbing with the gang. There are a lot of other nominees for flying wraith, but none a logical choice.

Thus grew the legend of the Dalton brothers, an abiding heartache to their long-suffering mother, an embarrassment to their honest siblings, and a plague upon the world of honest folk.

But they made for a bunch of pretty fair movie scripts.

CHAPTER 2

Empty Men

The Fleagles

Their names didn't become familiar in the way that the Daltons and the James boys did, but in their own way they were worse specimens of humankind, which is saying quite a lot. The Fleagle brothers flourished, if that's the word, in the early part of the twentieth century and, for a while, did very well at their adopted trade, the gentle art of bank robbery. One estimate puts the total of their loot in the neighborhood of a million dollars, in those days a very great deal of money indeed.

Among many other places, they raided the First National Bank of Ottawa, Kansas, a payday of an estimated two hundred thousand dollars. That job went like clockwork, at least from the Fleagles' point of view, although not everybody involved enjoyed it. As one customer put it: "The robbery . . . was thrilling, but she didn't crave it again."

Ralph and "Little Jake"—christened Jacob Henry—were Kansas boys who aspired to the big time as robbers and for a little while reached their dream. They formed their own gang and successfully pulled off several substantial holdups across the West and Midwest. And then, like most of their comrades in crime, they overreached, and their biggest payday also proved their undoing.

They hit the First National Bank in Lamar, Colorado, in May of 1928, and what they thought would be another bonanza went badly awry, in spite of the fact that they had cased the bank and made minute preparations, including maps of the local county roads. The brothers had two more professional robbers along for backup: George Abshier and Howard Royston.

They were all experienced hoodlums, and each knew his position and function. There was the usual waving of guns and shouting of threats and orders, and one customer was even shoved onto the floor. Everything should have gone smoothly. The technique had worked before and maybe it would have this time, except for the Lamar bank president, Amos Parrish.

Parrish was well along in years but made of stern stuff nevertheless, and so, when the brothers and two others announced loudly that this was a stickup, he reached for his friend "Betsy," an old single-action Colt .45, rumored to have once been carried by Frank James. With the Colt, he pulled down on the big bandit called Howard Royston. He hit the robber in the mouth with the first round. Parrish's next round misfired, and his third shot buried itself in the bank's ceiling.

And then Parrish was down and dying, and his son John—known as Jaddo—was headed for a closet where there was not only other weaponry but a telephone. He never made it, cut down by one of the Fleagle brothers. The gang fled then, making for their car with the badly wounded Royston and a bag of the bank's money.

They also took with them two hostages, bank employees Everett Kesinger and E. A. Lundgren, and ran for their hideout on a dilapidated Kansas farm.

Lundgren they released along the way, but they kept Kesinger, even though he pleaded with them that he was married and had a small child. Why they released one man and kept the other a prisoner remains a mystery . . . but it was the difference between life and death. Kesinger ended up dead, murdered by the gang in an abandoned shack near Liberal, Kansas.

They had gotten lots of money, all right—some two hundred thousand dollars—but when the smoke cleared in Lamar, the gang was on the run, dashing wildly for safety and pursued by the law. They would remain high on the wanted list, for they left two dead men behind them as they fled from Lamar, and there was more to come—much more.

That kind of killing of innocents would not be forgotten, nor would the kidnappings, and the hunt was on. County sheriff Lloyd Alderman vowed that he would never rest until the robbers were run down; he was as good as his word. For now, however, the law was frustrated.

After the Lamar robbery the sheriff had chased the robbers out of town for some miles, until his car was hit with long-range rifle fire by the gang. The lawman did not have the weaponry to return fire at that distance, for in those more innocent days, a service station attendant, cleaning up, had removed the lawman's rifle and neglected to put it back. And so the gang managed to break contact.

They could have quit while they were ahead. What they'd done so far was bad enough, but now they made it far worse. They murdered a man whose profession was healing and who had left his home to help one of them.

For Royston had been hard hit by the banker's Colt and obviously needed medical attention. And so the brothers visited a local doctor and fed him a cock-and-bull tale of a young boy whose foot had been crushed by a tractor. The good physician grabbed his bag and his car keys, and Jake went along with him, ostensibly to give him directions to his patient.

It was the last drive the doctor would ever make, of course, for once he had treated Royston, he became a liability in the eyes of the Fleagle boys. He, too, was murdered, shot in the head with a shotgun, his body dumped into a deep ravine and his car pushed after him. It was found only when sighted by a searching National Guard aircraft. The doctor had either been gratuitously beaten or had put up a fight on his last ride, for he was covered with bruises, one leg was broken, and he had sustained a murderous blow to the face.

The doctor was gone, but indirectly he would be the gang's nemesis. For, the story goes, on the way to see the "patient," Jake was apparently having trouble rolling down the window of the doctor's car. You have to pull it out at the top, said the doctor helpfully; Jake did so, and rolled the window down. That simple little action would get him killed.

All the rest of the car had been carefully wiped down before the car was pushed down the ravine . . . but nobody thought to wipe the top of a window. The single print was duly matched to one of Jake's, a considerable feat during the infancy of forensics.

"I'm going to bring these fellows down," said Sheriff Alderman to the police chief. The chief reached over to shake his hand, vowing, "I'm with you until you do it." And so it would be.

The Fleagle saga abounds in rumors, including one that casts their mother as a coconspirator and indeed the leader and planner of the gang's operations, "the brains of the whole Fleagle outfit . . . she'll pull the wool over your eyes," as one lawman put it. Shades of Ma Barker.

A competing rumor casts her husband as the evil genius, and his wife as a long-suffering Christian woman much put upon by the rest of her family. As Chief Richardson, who had arrested the senior Fleagle "often," is quoted as saying, "Look out for old Jake—he's likely to take a potshot at you." Another source said the family's neighbors feared them.

The law jailed father Fleagle and two more of his sons, and one of them was incautious enough to mention in a lawman's hearing that the pair awaited a message from still another brother, a message from Kankakee, Illinois. That city's police were asked to watch the post office and sure enough, Ralph turned up and asked for mail addressed to an alias.

Post office personnel called police, who arrested Ralph at a nearby bank, cashing a check of all things. He was arrested without incident and promptly rolled over on his confederates. His purpose was ostensibly to save his father and brothers from prosecution, but he also cut a favorable deal for himself, under which the district attorney agreed not to "ask for the death penalty" at Ralph's trial.

Ralph's information led very quickly to the arrest of Royston in San Andreas, California, and Abshier in Grand Junction, Colorado. Both men, and Ralph Fleagle, were tried in Colorado with appropriate due process of law. All three pleaded guilty to murder and robbery, and the jury's sentence was death for all of them. Ralph was horrified, protesting that he had a deal. "And we kept our word," said the DA. "We didn't ask for the death penalty." But the jury imposed the ultimate penalty anyway.

On appeal, the court agreed with the DA, and all three men were well and truly hanged. Jake wrote a letter to the governor trying to save his brother's worthless hide, alleging that the whole robbery was an "inside job" and that the younger Parrish had been killed by his father's weapon. Nobody bought this fairy tale for a moment, and Ralph swung like the others.

At least on their departure from this earth they had the dubious pleasure of trying out a novel device, popularly known as the "do-it-yourself-hanging-machine." This contraption was so called because once noose and blindfold were in place, the condemned man simply stepped forward onto a sort of little platform. That triggered a massive reaction from a collection of pulleys and weights, the notion being that the condemned man was jerked upward and his neck instantly broken. It usually worked. Usually.

This left on the loose only Jake, who evaded capture for a little more than two years. The law kept searching; after the bloodbath in Colorado, no officer was going to give up. And at last persistence paid off . . . that and a little guile. The law concocted a letter from an old Fleagle confederate—then in police custody—proposing a meeting for further "business."

Jake had been hiding out in a dilapidated chicken-ranch building in southern Missouri. All the officers knew where he was generally located because of the provenance of his letter to the state governor. They had enough information to narrow the number of post offices to which specious "general delivery" letters could be sent and the news-papers in which to advertise.

It worked. Jake wrote his onetime acquaintance he thought was the source of the phony letters. The law identified his handwriting, inter-cepted the letter, and answered it. Jake arranged to meet his acquain-tance in Yellville, Arkansas, and planned to rob a bank in that little town. Take a "Frisco" train to Aurora, Missouri, wrote Jake, change for Yellville, and meet me there.

Jake decided to board the train at peaceful Branson, Missouri, a friendly spot tucked away in the Ozarks, just above the Arkansas line. Today the town sits on beautiful Table Rock Lake, and it's a mecca for tourists. In Jake's day, back in October of 1930, the lake hadn't been built yet, and the countryside was still very much quiet and peaceful. The lawmen were ahead of Jake again and waiting in force, some on the train itself, others in the station.

According to the *Los Angeles Evening Herald*, some twenty-three postal inspectors, city detectives, and deputy sheriffs were present in and around little Branson. After Jake got on the train and found a seat, the law moved in. Jake made a terminal mistake and went for his pistol. Taken to the hospital in Springfield, he died the next day, and the world was a little safer. He was just forty years old, which a good many people thought was about forty too many.

Jake did have one lasting claim to fame. There is a story that he was the inspiration for Evil Eye Fleegle, an Al Capp character created for *Li'l Abner*. Evil Eye, as amoral as his namesake, attacked people he didn't like with his devastating stare—the "double whammy"—with a triple whammy in reserve for special cases. At least that dubious fame lived after Jake; he couldn't take along the money.

Jake Fleagle AUTHOR'S COLLECTION

The *Herald's* front page waxed positively eloquent about Jake's demise: "His gun pumping a futile rain of bullets and his lips twisted in a defiant snarl, 'Little Jake' Fleagle, leader and lone survivor of the notorious Fleagle 'Wolf Pack' of western bandits and killers, was wounded, probably fatally. . . ."

Fleagle had fallen to a bullet fired by Los Angeles police detective lieutenant Harry Wilde, one of at least three LA officers present at the kill. According to the paper, one of Wilde's colleagues had grabbed Fleagle's gun hand while Wilde cut the outlaw down. Fleagle's "futile rain" of bullets—however many that really was—didn't hit anybody, but Wilde's return fire put a round in Jake's gut.

The small army of lawmen had been after Little Jake for five months, along with police and postal inspectors from many other places. The paper added that when Fleagle tried to shoot it out with the law, there were a total of eight officers actually on the train, and others in the area of the station.

The *Herald* opined that Fleagle's wound was "probably" fatal, and added that if he lived, he would surely hang like Royston, Abshier, and his brother, for what the paper somewhat grandiloquently called "the most cold-blooded murders since the James and Youngers rode wild." The paper was right on the first count, for the doctors could not save Fleagle. And the *Herald's* second point was almost surely correct as well. No Colorado jury would have spent much time debating Jake's sentence.

So passed the Fleagle brothers, empty men with nothing inside but consuming self-interest. We'd call them sociopaths today. Back in the 1920s, people used other terms to describe such trash. Most were unprintable, but certainly accurate.

Like a good many other criminals, the Fleagles' career on the wrong side of the law produced much mythology. But it also gave birth to some self-conscious poetry:

> It was here on the old station platform
> where Jake Fleagle made his last stand,
> But one fatal shot from the sheriff,
> And once more the law got its man.

> Oh, why are these young men so foolish,
> To think they can murder at will,
> When there is that mighty commandment,
> That teaches us "thou shalt not kill."

And a great deal more in the same vein—about the only epitaph Jake Fleagle was going to get.

CHAPTER 3

Two Banks at Once

Disaster at Northfield

No robber gang of any period is more famous than the James-Younger gang. They have been the subject of countless fanciful films, mostly casting them as something akin to Robin Hood and His Merry Men, with Jesse, of course, as Robin.

They were anything but.

Even the well-acted James-Younger films have been wildly inaccurate. The best of them was the epic called *The Great Northfield Minnesota Raid*, which had a fine cast, but even it slid off into the world of invention, casting a bunch of tough, honest Northfield citizens as cowardly and crooked, and it had the bankers embezzling from their depositors, both notions wholly without factual support. The films went sharply downhill from there, ending in the worst Western film ever made, *Jesse James Meets Frankenstein's Daughter*. The less said about that epic the better.

Jesse James, as guerrilla LIBRARY OF CONGRESS, LC-USZ62-38555

In fact the Northfield bank raid marked the end of the road for the most famous gang in history, thanks to the courage of the whole population and in particular of a very honest, devoted cashier, whose loyalty to his employer and his depositors cost him his life.

Both sets of brothers were survivors of the vicious border conflict of the Civil War. They were members of Missouri Bushwhacker gangs, followers of such scum as William Quantrill, William "Bloody Bill" Anderson, and their ilk. Where most survivors of these guerrilla bands went home after the war and turned to peaceful pursuits, the Jameses and Youngers did not. They became one of the most successful outlaw gangs in American history.

The families were no strangers to violence, for they lived in a violent time. The father of the Younger clan, Thomas Coleman Younger, was murdered in 1862 while riding back from Kansas City with a considerable supply of cash. The killing was the work of a band of so-called federal militia, whose leader was later arrested for the crime by a Union general.

And the family also lost one brother along the way, John, killed by a Pinkerton agent in a shootout in the spring of 1874. Part of the endless mythology created by books about the time includes the assertion by one writer that John didn't die at all, but showed up later in Fort Smith as none other than "hanging judge" Isaac Parker, ignoring that fact that Judge Parker was well known as a political figure as early as 1864.

The Hollywood nonsense aside, the James-Younger gang was in fact a deadly, resourceful outlaw band. For years they got away with murder—literally—and much robbery. They are even sometimes credited with being the first of the train robbers, although they weren't. That dubious distinction belongs to still another criminal family—the Reno boys—who also get some space later in this book.

The stories about the James-Younger gang's exploits are myriad, and some are even true. They've been repeatedly characterized as benevolent bandits, robbing the rich to give to the poor. What they were was far simpler: common thieves and killers . . . but highly successful ones.

Part of the baggage that typically goes with outlaw success is arrogance, and maybe that's what led the gang to Minnesota. Or maybe one of their men was from that neck of the woods; or maybe, as has been suggested, the gang was going to carry the war into the heart of "Yankee country"; or maybe the owner of the bank was a former Union officer, still another story. Whatever their reasoning, as it turned out the trip north was not at all a good idea.

The Minnesota trip at first looked like a pure pleasure jaunt. They indulged in some frivolity with various ladies, drank some beer, saw the sights, and even went to a baseball game. But then, when the time finally came for business, they went to the quiet, small town of Northfield, a peaceful place where nobody carried a gun.

There they made the same mistakes the Dalton boys would make later in little Coffeyville: They stuck out, riding fine horses and armed to the teeth. They immediately aroused suspicion, and their labored attempts to look innocent and casual fooled nobody.

Three of them went into the bank, including both Jesse and Frank James, while two more waited in the street outside, Cole Younger pretending to adjust a saddle girth that didn't need it. The other three waited nearby, just across a little bridge. Their function was to be the tried-and-true gang tactic of "hoorahing" the town: galloping down the street yelling at the citizens to get inside and firing their revolvers in the air. The idea was to terrify the citizenry so that no coherent resistance would ever organize.

The tactic had worked well many times before. In Northfield it didn't.

Inside the bank, the gang threatened and blustered, but got nowhere. They didn't believe the gutsy cashier's invention of a locked vault, but they weren't bright enough to pull on the vault doors . . .

which were, in fact, open. They couldn't even manage to find the cash drawer, which was right in front of them.

They might have had a little more time to get it right, but the owner of a local hardware store had spotted the gang members for what they were. What with their good horses, their weaponry, and their long dusters, no wonder the hardware man said, "I believe they're here to rob the bank." He even tried to follow the three inside men into the bank building.

Dense gang member Clel Miller pulled a gun on the hardware man and warned him against going inside; and then, when the businessman ran off down the street yelling that the bank was being robbed, Miller took a shot at him. He missed, but he did ensure that anyone who hadn't known already that something was wrong at the bank surely knew now.

People near the bank ran in all directions, and men who could find firearms used them. Inside, the cashier was wantonly shot down, although he had done nothing threatening to the three outlaws in front of him. The identity of the killer is not known for certain, but in all probability it was Frank James. Another townsman was murdered on the street; his only sin was that he spoke little English and probably did not understand shouted orders from the hoorahing outlaws to "get in, get in!"

The reaction of the townspeople, seen by the outlaws as "stupid squareheads," was nothing short of ferocious. Clel Miller went down with a fatal wound, as did fellow outlaw Bill Stiles. All of the Younger boys and Charlie Pitts were hit, and in all probability so was Frank James. Three unarmed citizens even stood together on the street hurling rocks at the bewildered bandits, yelling "stone 'em, stone 'em!" Bells clanged and dogs barked all over town, adding to the din of gunfire, the shouts of the fighters, and the cries of the wounded.

The most famous outlaw gang of the day was soundly whipped, and they knew it. They stood not upon the order of their going, but galloped for such safety as there was. They had not done anything like a preraid reconnaissance, however—another colossal stupidity—and so they spent days miserably wandering around strange territory, hurt and hungry, with only the vaguest notion of where they were or how to reach safety. And while they wandered, parties totaling as many as a thousand men searched diligently for what was left of the gang.

The James boys at last abandoned the other four, who were run down by a small posse from the town of Madelia. These gallant citizens waded into a dense thicket after these famous hoodlums, and they won the ensuing point-blank firefight hands down, killing Charlie Pitts and wounding and capturing the three Younger boys.

The Youngers would have the chance to learn from their mistakes; they could use the many years they spent in a Minnesota prison to mull over what went wrong. And by the time they got out, they were old men, no longer the flamboyant princes of outlawry.

As for the others, they went on to useful careers in public service . . . as dissection cadavers at the university medical school. It was probably the best thing they ever did for other people.

As everybody knows, Jesse James got himself shot by Bob Ford, who went on the lecture circuit for a while, boasting about the killing. Later, he opened a saloon in booming Creede, Colorado; there Bob was himself shot quite dead a while later by a no-good named O'Kelly, who still later got crossways with a tough Oklahoma City policeman and came in second, dead last as it were. Cole Younger and Frank James survived all of this and went on the road with a "crime does not pay" routine. After all the miles and all the blood and misery, both of them died in bed.

The Northfield affair, indeed the gang's whole career in outlawry, was grist for an endless series of sensational publications replete with drawings of robbery, shootings, corpses, and general lawlessness. For example, something called *Young Men of America, A Sparkling Journal for Young Gentlemen*, offered several pages on "The Younger Boys, or,

On left is the bank held up by Frank and Jesse James, Cole, Jim and Bob Younger and others, in Northfield, Minn., Sept. 7, 1876, for which the Youngers served time in Stillwater pen.

Northfield bank WESTERN HISTORY COLLECTIONS, UNIVERSITY OF OKLAHOMA LIBRARY

the Fiends of the Border." It opened with a full-page drawing of a couple of nondescript men brandishing pistols and looking threatening.

There were lots of these potboilers, and the mythology went on from there, filling books and grubby pamphlets with varying degrees of inaccuracy. Then when the movies got into the act, the unreality got even worse. Maybe nobody in Hollywood can read a history book.

CHAPTER 4

Massacre in Greene County

The Youngs

The names of the Young brothers aren't widely known, but they should be, for Harry and Jennings Young had far more blood on their hands than most of their more famous contemporaries. They were authors of the single biggest disaster for law officers in the history of that hazardous profession.

The brothers came from a large farm family that settled in near the embryonic town of Frederick in newly opened Tillman County, Oklahoma, back in 1902. They had come down from Ozark, Missouri, for a fresh start by "proving up" their 160 acres, a weary and laborious process aptly called "heartbreak farming." Besides parents James (called J. D.) and Willie Florence, there were seven kids, with three more to come. Sons Paul and Jennings were old enough to help with the farming, but they proved to be unenthusiastic.

The Youngs made it work, however, and finally sold out in August 1917, for fifteen thousand dollars, a substantial chunk of money in that time and place. They moved back to Christian County, Missouri, from whence they came. Paul and Jennings were already practicing their criminal skills, burglarizing a business in Nixa, along with two more in Ozark, the county seat, and possibly several more. They weren't very good at it and got ten years apiece, of which they served about five.

The *Leader*, a paper in nearby Springfield, commented on the fact that the eyebrows of the two met in a continuous line across their faces, a fact in which, the paper said, "Devotees of the art of criminology will be interested. . . ."

If their eyebrows were a sign of hereditary criminal behavior, the brothers proved it, next accused of robbing a railroad boxcar—a federal offense—along with brother Oscar and their own mother. In the end, only Jennings was convicted, and he was sentenced to three years in Leavenworth.

Father J. D. was dead by now, maybe of a broken heart. Wife Willie and daughter Florence defended—successfully—a civil action over a used car, and there was also an accusation against Willie and two of her daughters, a matter which was never tried. In the end, Willie sold the family farm, and the price of the property at least paid all the expenses, lawyer's fees and the like.

Meanwhile, in 1924, brother Paul had gotten himself in trouble for burglary down in Texas. That got him ten years in Huntsville prison, and it also produced the illuminating news that he was missing three toes, which his mother said he had shot off himself to avoid the 1918 draft.

Paul was lucky. The governor of Texas was then the celebrated "Ma" Ferguson, famous for pardoning all manner of jailbirds, and Paul got a pardon in 1925. It was "witnessed" by Ma's husband, who had also been governor of Texas, whose administration was surrounded—as was Ma's—by accusations of corruption.

Harry (christened Lyman Harry) Young had started out on the wrong side of the law by the time he was twenty-one, when he was arrested for the first act of his career in crime. The court had mercy, and he remained free, but he hungered for more. And so, in a period of a year, he was charged with a series of offenses of ever-increasing severity. The result was a three-year sentence handed down in a Greene County, Missouri, court.

That was the spring of 1927, and Harry, like his brothers, hadn't learned a thing. For in 1929 he killed officer Mark Noe, firing three rounds, two of which hit Noe in the head; at least one round made the murder seem suspiciously like a premeditated execution. Later on Willie, ever the defensive mother hen, asserted that Noe was killed when his own gun fell on the car floor and shot him; her poor mistreated son didn't do a thing, etc., ad nauseam. For the moment, Harry had disappeared, maybe working in Houston.

The latter was possible, since in 1930 brother Jennings was also in Texas, again in the slammer, this time in Fort Worth, accused of several car thefts, at least one of them committed out of state. His conviction got him two years in Leavenworth, and when he got out, he headed back to the old ways and old days, back in Greene County, where Mama Willie was trying to keep the family's present farm afloat. The task was really beyond her, although the ground was good. Her sons weren't much help, not only because they were profoundly unenthusiastic, but also because they spent a lot of their days in prison or on the run.

But at the end of December 1931, Jennings and Harry arrived at the family farm. Jennings had been out of Leavenworth only a little over a month. They came without notice, and about the same time their sister Lorena arrived with her family, her husband immediately announcing that they wouldn't have come at all had they known the brothers were also there.

Harry and Jennings lost no time. They stole a car, and when they had some trouble selling it, they got Lorena and sister Vinita to help them. The car dealer smelled a rat—he was wary of anything to do with the Young family—and called in the police. And so the next day, when the women returned to the dealership to get their money, two officers were waiting for them.

In the interim, Harry had visited the nearby farm of brother Oscar to borrow two guns "to go hunting." Jennings was at odds with both Oscar and his wife, so the lying was left to Harry. As to their prowess with the guns, rumor made the brothers into modern-day William Tells. As the *Springfield Press* said of Harry, he could throw marbles in the air, "shooting them in two with a small caliber rifle." Why, sure he could, and probably also leap tall buildings with a single bound.

But he got the weapons, a 12-gauge shotgun and a little .25-20 rifle. Both weapons were semiautomatic, providing considerable firepower. Both brothers also had handguns.

The law was still searching for the brothers, and among other things, officers closely watched the rest of the family. And so, when the two sisters went to deliver the hot car and get paid, the law nabbed them and took them down to the city jail, where they later brought mother Willie as well. In time, the daughters admitted their brothers were at the family homestead, and the law prepared to make the long-awaited arrest. Partly as a matter of protocol, the posse included not only the city police, who had primary jurisdiction, but also officers from the sheriff's department. There was even one civilian, apparently just along simply for the thrill.

All told, there was a total of ten officers, but what they had in manpower they lacked in armament. Nobody brought along anything but a handgun, save a couple of gas grenades one officer thought to include. Nor was there much ammunition, apparently no more than the few cartridges each man routinely carried.

Unprepared, they ran into a hornet's nest.

Getting no answer to their knocks, they at last elected to kick in a door, and they chose the back one. First, they tried a gas grenade, which bounced futilely off the window frame. Next, the crash as they smashed open the kitchen door was answered by a shotgun blast that hit the county sheriff squarely in the chest. A second shot tore another officer's face apart and lodged in a third man's shoulder.

The officers returned the fire with their handguns but quickly began to run out of ammunition. Another lawman was hit in the ankle and still another officer, also out of cartridges and peering out from behind his sheltering maple tree, took a rifle bullet squarely in the forehead. A seventh officer had his brains blown out by that deadly shotgun.

The remaining officers ran to take shelter in the barn. In the process, Officer Tony Oliver took two rifle rounds; the second killed him. Meanwhile, obeying an order to "go for help and ammunition," Detective Virgil Johnson jumped into a police car with another officer and the civilian straphanger and roared off toward town as fire from the house shattered his windshield. The remaining two officers on the scene, both also out of ammunition, running and dodging bullets, managed to reach a nearby road.

That left nobody to besiege the house, and before Johnson could get back with reinforcements, the two Young brothers had collected a pile of police handguns and disappeared. An intensive search went on around the area, conducted first by a disorganized mob of volunteers, and within a couple of hours by a National Guard artillery battery from Springfield. Somebody started to set fire to the house, but Constable Curtis stopped it, shouting that the house might have evidence in it, and anyhow, the outlaws had fled.

They sure had. Somehow they made it the six or so miles to Springfield, where they stole a car and drove south. The car turned up in Streetman, Texas, some 170 miles from Houston, where it had been run off the road. A Good Samaritan on horseback stopped to help the two men in it. He told them there wasn't a wrecker close by but said he'd get his team of mules and pull the car to his nearby farm. When he returned with his team, however, the two men were gone. Only then did he notice not only a rifle and shotgun in the car, but that the license plates had been torn off and thrown into the field. He called the police and then the hunt turned toward Houston. Why the brothers left the weapons behind is unknown, though it was probably simply to avoid attracting attention when they abandoned the wrecked car. Whatever the reason, it would turn out to be a fatal mistake.

The pursuit attracted hundreds of grim-faced lawmen: Six of their fellow officers were dead, and three more were wounded. Among other things, their widespread search turned up several stolen cars in the Young family's barn; two of them had been stolen in Texas. Ma Young and her two daughters remained in jail, where, of course, they couldn't resist talking to the press.

And so the search centered in the Houston vicinity, involving hundreds of police, some of whom were posted along the Rio Grande to head off any escape into Mexico. A salesman turned up who had given the brothers a ride as far as Streetman, and the police reasoned that the brothers had gone on to Houston.

They had, and there they made still another mistake, when Harry approached an employee of a Houston paper, asking for a "midnight edition." He wanted, he said, to read about those "Missouri killers." He got his paper, but looking at pictures in a later edition, the employee discovered the man was one of those very fugitives.

The police got their final break when a Houston resident rented a room in his home to two men; it wasn't long before he looked at the paper and discovered who at least one of his new lodgers was. He called police, who sent in a squad of handpicked officers who were well armed with shotguns and rifles, and carrying tear gas grenades as well. This time the tables were turned from the massacre at the farm, for their quarry had only the pistols taken from the dead officers.

The officers summoned the brothers to surrender but were answered by gunshots. They returned the fire, and at last the lawmen heard four more shots inside the brothers' room. Finally a voice called out to them, "come on in, we're dead." The officers took no chances, but pumped the room full of tear gas and waited patiently until it cleared before they entered.

There wasn't any danger from the vicious Young boys, and now there never would be again. One was dead, the other dying, and the general opinion was that they had stood face-to-face and killed each other rather than fall into the hands of the officers. There was evidence that Jennings had been shot no less than seven times, and that Harry had absorbed two .44 slugs, allegedly from Jennings's revolver.

Some veteran officers doubted the mutual suicide theory, pointing out that it was unlikely two men could absorb that kind of punishment and still blast away at each other point-blank so many times. Still, the routine postmortem medical exam listed the cause of death of both brothers as "murder."

There were also the inevitable rumors that some of those bullet holes in the Young corpses were the work of the lawmen . . . but then, the public generally didn't care very much one way or the other, as long as the brothers were history. Rather more exciting was news that one of the lawmen involved in the first battle thought he saw the notorious Fred Barker inside the house. He hadn't, but it made a good story.

There was no end to the questions left unanswered: How did the brothers leave the area? On foot? In a car hidden nearby? How did their bag of pistols get to Texas? Was somebody else with them in the farmhouse? Did they have help in fleeing, and if so, who helped when and how? One story alleged that five stolen cars were recovered from the Young farm, four of which had been stolen down in Texas.

There was such excitement in the wake of the tragedy that the undertaker charged with transporting the mortal remains of the dead brothers was dogged by the curious, to the point that he had to change his plans, driving a different route and taking complex precautions to protect the brothers' bodies. At one point he removed all door and window handles on his hearse to avoid outside interference with the bodies.

There remained the rest of the family.

Oscar and his wife—generally called "Mrs. Oscar"—were charged as accessories to murder, because the guns used in the crimes belonged to Oscar. That charge was soon dropped, which left the two sisters charged with receiving stolen property, specifically the stolen car they had tried to peddle for their brothers.

Poor old Willie was also charged with receiving stolen property, in her case clothing burgled by her sons, which was found in her sons' luggage. That charge also was ended by the DA's *nolle prosequi*. But the old lady was distraught on learning that her treasured sons had murdered six lawman and wounded two more.

"Oh my God!" she said. "What am I to do now? Daddy's in heaven. I'm glad Daddy didn't even know about this." Which sentiment was accompanied by a lament for "my teeth," which she had somehow managed to break. Willie wanted her daughter Vinita—then in another jail—to help her get them fixed.

Willie's woes were not over, for her no-good son Oscar was charged with transporting a stolen car. Willie was charged with the same offense, but the charges against her were ultimately dismissed. Not so for Oscar, who got four years in Leavenworth. Almost immediately after his release, he was charged with larceny from the US mail and got three more years. This was Oscar's ninth dose of hard time—or maybe his tenth—but he appears to have finally learned something, or perhaps he just got tired of the fast life. It was his last trip to the pen.

Nobody will ever know exactly the involvement of the rest of the family in the monstrous sins of Harry, Jennings, and Oscar, or in the other offenses alleged against various member of the family. They were a clannish bunch, and so the inclination of all or most of them would be to help each other out. Some Springfield newspapermen, in a little book written not long after the event, may have described the family ethos pretty accurately.

Their clannish nature might have gotten a good deal worse, the journalists reasoned, after the family moved from the Ozarks down into Oklahoma. The family, especially Willie, seems to have resented many of their neighbors. The Youngs appear to have felt that they were somehow superior to the locals. As a clan, they also disliked and mistrusted authority. In short, to those around them, the family presented "a compact, solid, impenetrable front . . . there are none who raise the voice of protest against the depredations of a brother."

Memories of the Young boys lingered on. People wrote songs and poems about the brothers and their crimes, generally adhering more or less closely to the truth, although at least one inexplicably praised them as "brave and gallant men." Even today you can order a whole CD of songs about these scumbags, their exploits, and their bitter end. Folklore dies hard.

As for Willie, she found a little peace at last. For with the help of a daughter, the farm was sold and the bills paid. Willie was installed in a house in town, where she did some babysitting and took in lodgers. She lived on until the summer of 1945, and died at age seventy-eight.

She is buried next to Daddy.

CHAPTER 5

Debacle on the Border

The Christian Boys Panic at Nogales

Most criminals today are not very bright, which is why so many of them end up in prison. The intellectual caliber of western bad men wasn't any higher, which not only got lots of them a trip to jail, but lots more a one-way trip to Boot Hill. Along the way they committed some successful crimes; a lot more often they got nothing but egg on their faces. Thus with the "High Fives": the Christian brothers and their entourage.

Lots of Arizona criminals were imports, usually men who left someplace else for their health. They were often in a very great hurry, with the law close behind them, and their back trail liberally salted with corpses, hurt people, missing stock, and empty cash bags. The Christian boys were just such émigrés, products of Oklahoma Territory.

The Christians, brothers Bill and Bob, traveled with their family from Texas into the wide-open land north of the Canadian River in 1891. In what was to become Pottawatomie County, Oklahoma Territory, this wild-and-woolly area was studded with "saloon towns," dreary collections of shanties like Young's Crossing, Keokuk Falls, Violet Springs, and The Corner, a tiny patch of land on the South Canadian River whose collection of sleazy saloons attracted trash from miles in every direction.

The down-at-heels bars were easy places in which to get killed, entirely aside from the noxious rotgut they served. Keokuk Falls' booze parlors, for example, were quaintly known as the "seven deadly saloons." At The Corner lived a dedicated doctor named Mooney, whose practice included treating a wide assortment of gunshots, knifings, and bloody batteries. The good doctor once managed an amputation on a saloon table while a drunk held a lamp to light the doctor's work and the usual revelry continued all around him.

In Keokuk Falls somebody murdered a saloon keeper named Haning. The killer shot Haning in the head, left him on the floor of his bar, then came back, "between daybreak and sunrise," to finish the process by the unusual expedient of driving a rusty nail into Haning's ear. When trains of the Choctaw, Oklahoma and Gulf Railroad stopped in Shawnee, the conductor comfortingly announced: "Shawnee! Twenty minutes for lunch and to see a man killed!"

In all of these dreary settlements like Shawnee, John Barleycorn flowed in floods until all of Oklahoma went dry in 1907. At the turn of the century, the Pottawatomie country boasted more than sixty saloons and two distilleries, and the town of Shawnee's *daily* booze intake in 1903 was said to be twenty-five gallons of whiskey and seven hundred gallons of beer.

The Pottawatomie country was a natural shelter for both inept amateur robbers like Al Jennings and career outlaws such as the Daltons, Bill Doolin, Zip Wyatt, and a pair of young hoodlums called the Casey boys, whom we'll meet again. With Indian Territory on two sides, the country was a haven for the bootleggers who ran hooch into

36

the Indian lands. It was here that the venerable term "bootlegger" may have had its genesis, describing those smugglers who rode into Indian country with pint bottles of prime rotgut stuffed into the tops of their boots.

Oddly, the area was also known as a "fine country for the poor man," where crops grew well and game abounded. Good people lived here, too, and one little town was named "Moral," for its first citizen decreed no booze would be tolerated in his peaceful community. The Anti-Horse Thief Association did what it could to curb widespread rustling, decreeing that all horses must be branded with a "c" on the left jaw and have papers. Any man who rode a branded horse without carrying the proper papers was facing a vast amount of trouble.

The Christian family was considered respectable, but by the time the brothers reached their twenties, they had an unenviable reputation as whiskey runners and horse thieves. Back then, the Christian boys headquartered in a saloon in Violet Springs run by one Andy Morrison—eventually murdered while sleeping in his own back room—and in April of 1895 the brothers graduated to murder.

It came to pass one day that the brothers and a drinking buddy, one John Mackey, walked out of Doug Barnes's saloon and found the law waiting for them in the form of Deputy Will Turner (or Turney). Turner had warrants for the brothers' arrest, but he made the terminal mistake of trying to make the arrest alone. Turner probably didn't count on the brothers and Mackey all drawing on him at once. He died in the dusty street.

Tough Sheriff W. B. "Billy" Trousdale ran down Mackey, and the Christian boys turned themselves in, which turned out to be a bad idea. The court reporter on the case remembered that a "horde of people attended from the Four Corners District, and were about the hardest looking lot in my experience." Disreputable audience or not, however, the brothers were convicted.

One story relates that the county judge on the case was J. D. F. Jennings, who is said to have been upset at the Christians because they had killed a friend of his famous son Al, one of Oklahoma's more celebrated and inept outlaws. Or maybe the judge just didn't like murderers. Whatever his mood, according to this story he gave the Christian boys life sentences and shipped them off to the Oklahoma City jail to await transport to prison.

However, another story—probably the correct one—says the boys were tried and sentenced by Judge Henry Scott, and the court reporter remembered that Judge Scott gave the brothers twenty-five and twenty-two years for the killing. The Oklahoma City *Daily Oklahoman*, however, told its readers that the Christians had been sentenced to eight and ten years. In later days Jennie Cantelou, the court reporter, remembered the sentences as quite lenient, recalling, perhaps inaccurately, that the deputy had been "killed from ambush."

After sentencing, whatever their terms actually were, the pair was transferred to the Oklahoma County Jail in Oklahoma City, then a two-story building fitted out with interior steel cages and thought to be a solid, secure lockup. Confined at the same time, in the same cell, was a nineteen-year-old bad hat called Casey, who with his brother had murdered Deputy Sheriff Sam Farris over in Canadian County in the latter part of May.

One Casey brother—either Jim or Vic depending on what account you read—had been shot up in the fight with the deputy and later died. But the surviving brother—the *Daily Oklahoman* said it was Vic—was going to stand trial for murder. He was due to be released on bond, but apparently he did not care to wait.

Since neither he nor the Christians wanted any part of prison, Bob prevailed upon Jessie Finlay, his girlfriend, to smuggle in several guns, which he stashed in the stovepipe inside his cell. The outlaws chose Sunday, June 30, 1895, to make their break, for on Sundays the jailer, J. H. Garver, allowed his prisoners to wander about freely in the corridor outside their cells. Garver was either unusually easygoing or just plain negligent. Only the day before the break, a Pottawatomie County lawman had wired him, warning about the jailbreak. Garver did exactly nothing.

At first the break went well. Casey and the Christians pistol-whipped the jailer and ran into an alley behind the jail. There one of the Christians—probably Bill—stole a horse belonging to Police Chief Milt Jones and galloped out of town. The other brother—probably Bob—and Casey fled on foot, stopped a couple in a buggy and shoved their pistols into the driver's face. Carpenter Gus White, the driver, would not give up the reins, and he managed to pull the horses to a halt. Although the fugitives shot White in the leg and the stomach, he would survive.

Chief Jones was closing in, but as he got within eight or ten feet of the buggy, one of the outlaws turned and shot him down. Some observers thought Christian killed the lawman, but the coroner's jury decided Casey was the killer. Whoever fired the fatal shot, the officer staggered onto the sidewalk and sank down against a building. He was dead in five minutes.

A wild gun battle then broke out on Grand Avenue, the fugitives on one side and a couple of police officers and several armed citizens on the other. Bob Christian was hit, and the lawmen drilled Casey with bullets through the neck and head, whereof he expired in White's riddled buggy. The Christians quickly ran for their lives.

With Chief Jones lying dead in the street and both of the Christian brothers vanished, Oklahoma City reacted angrily, and a posse of "infuriated citizens" galloped after the outlaws. The *Daily Oklahoman* opined that there was "little doubt" the fugitives would be captured. "Should they be caught," the paper editorialized, "a double lynching will surely follow."

It was a fine idea and might well have come to pass, for the citizenry of Oklahoma City were indeed furious. One journalist accurately described the Christians as "noted thugs and desperadoes," and another, having viewed Casey at the undertaker's emporium, somewhat spitefully wrote that Casey "looked much better in death than in life," which may have indeed been true. But to do the justice everybody hungered for, the law first had to catch the Christians—that would prove very tough, though posses searched high and low.

The authorities soon established that a number of people had been part of the planning for the escape. Jessie, the loyal girlfriend, spent fourteen months in jail for her part in the break. Jailer Garver discovered that he should have paid attention to the warning wire: His negligence got him ten years in prison, and he served two before he was pardoned. Ironically, his incompetence would surprise nobody; the sheriff had planned to fire him the Monday after the break.

Two other probable conspirators, John Fessenden and Louis Miller, were riding with the brothers in the newly formed Christian gang. The most surprising conspirator was W. H. "Bill" Carr, an old-time deputy US marshal, whom authorities charged with supplying Bob's paramour with the very gun Carr had taken away from Bob when he arrested the outlaw. Carr got out on bond, but before his trial he "gave leg bail," as the saying went, left town abruptly, and was seen no more.

Not so the Christian brothers. They were on the run, but during the next couple of months they embarked on a string of raids on country post offices and general stores. It was bush-league, nickel-and-dime thievery, although it kept the countryside in an uproar. They even managed to bungle a robbery of the Wewoka Trading Company, called the "richest institution in the Seminole nation." They got only a couple of hundred dollars in "provisions and equipment," because the only man who knew the safe combination had gone home for dinner. Other raids on local stores followed, until, on the ninth of August, the gang ran into an ambush near the hamlet of Wilburton.

A deputy marshal killed Fessenden, and gang member Foster Holbrook was captured. On August 21, John Reeves—one of those who had furnished weaponry for the Oklahoma City jailbreak—was arrested near the town of Paoli. Later tried as a conspirator in Chief Jones's murder, he was sentenced to life.

On August 23 the Christians shot their way past lawmen west of Purcell; although Deputy Marshal W. E. Hocker was wounded in the fight, the posse believed Hocker had gotten a bullet into Bob Christian. In the small hours of September 30, Louis Miller—another of the jailbreak conspirators—was jumped by lawmen near Violet Springs. Miller decided to fight but wasn't good enough.

The gang reappeared in Oklahoma County in early September, breaking into the railroad agent's quarters in Edmond. And on October 6, they held up a St. Louis and San Francisco train east of Wilburton but rode off with only another measly haul. Their last hurrah came in December, when they robbed a mining company store in Coalgate, down in Choctaw country. This raid was another flop: a little more than two hundred dollars in money, plus "goods to the value of some $200."

Oklahoma had just gotten too hot for the Christian boys. A month or so later, they turned up in Billy the Kid country, Seven Rivers, New Mexico, and soon ended up in Arizona's Sulphur Springs Valley. By this time, Bill was calling himself Ed Williams, while brother Bob adopted the handle of Tom Anderson.

Bill went to work breaking horses for the 4-Bar ranch and soon acquired the nicknames of "202"—maybe from his weight—and "Black Jack," from his dark hair and mustache (not to be confused with Black Jack Ketchum, for whom Christian was and is sometimes mistaken). His partner, an honest cowboy named Ed Wilson, said of Christian, "A finer partner never lived. Big strong, fearless and good natured . . . ever ready to take his part, no matter what the game might be."

Black Jack loved to whoop it up over in the mining town of Bisbee, along the Mexican border, and Wilson recounted that the big puncher "could spend more money than fifteen men could earn." He often said, according to Wilson, that "he had a good idea to get up [an] outfit and go train robbing." He repeatedly urged Wilson to join him, but that honest cowpoke refused.

Others did not, however, and Christian soon raised another gang, including Texan Code (or Cole) Young, whose real name was probably Harris. Then there was Bob Hayes, who may have been another Texan, or maybe he was in fact an Iowa hoodlum named Sam Hassels.

Other gang members included George Musgrave, another Texan (who also called himself Jeff Davis and Jesse Johnson) who was an able career criminal. Then there was Jesse Williams (who may have been just another one of Musgrave's many aliases). Finally, add "Tom Anderson," who was probably brother Bob Christian, and you have the gang known in the southwest as the "High Fives," after a card game popular at the time.

All of these ne'er-do-wells, according to cowboy Wilson, were "crack shots," who removed the triggers from their pistols and simply thumbed back the hammer "when in a tight place" and fanned the pistol. "The speed," said Wilson, "with which they could shoot in this manner was simply amazing" (no doubt, but could they hit anything farther than ten feet away?).

With these trusty henchmen, and another hard case called Three-Fingered Jack Dunlap—later extinguished by tough lawman Jeff Milton—on the sixth of August, 1896, Black Jack rode off to rob the bank at Nogales, right on the border. Some of his band stayed outside with the horses; the others—probably Jesse Williams and Bob Hayes—went into the bank. They had excellent luck at first—their mouths must have watered at the sight of some thirty thousand dollars in hard money, counted out and waiting for a local rancher closing a stock purchase.

Right after that, however, things quickly began to come unstuck. According to one tale, the bank's directors were meeting upstairs;

hearing a commotion beneath, they threw open windows and opened fire on the astonished robbers. Another story says the rout of the bandits was begun by an act of God; a passing whirlwind slammed the bank's back door and scared the gang's inside men out of a year's growth, whereupon they decamped in a great hurry.

More probably, as other versions relate, the problem was a single tough bank man, probably clerk Frank Herrera. Whoever he was, he was all wool and a yard wide. Alone in the bank, he still snatched a pistol and began to blaze away. He didn't hit anybody, but his heroics were enough to drive the bandits pell-mell out into the street without their loot.

To add to their woes, either just before or just after the bank's resident hero started shooting, a passerby also pulled his .41 Colt and opened fire on the confused robbers. This was customs collector Frank King, a very tough cookie indeed.

Whatever the sequence of events really was, what with slamming doors and folks shooting at them, these big tough he-men quickly concluded that Nogales was no place to hang around. The inside men tumbled out of the bank in a great swivet, and the gang left their loot and fled, as cowboys said, at the high lope. The bank man was still firing behind them, though all he hit was the bank ceiling and an unfortunate horse parked across the street from the bank.

Frank King pursued the robbers, first on a buggy horse, then on a pony requisitioned from a passing cowboy, turning back only when the outlaws began to shoot at him. Not daunted, King then raised a posse and pursued, but to no avail. Other posses took the field as well, including Bisbee riders led by Burt Alvord, soon to leave the side of the law to become a bandit in his own right.

Sheriff Bob Leatherwood's party, with Alvord and Cochise County's pioneer photographer-turned-sheriff Camillus Fly along, got very near the outlaws. The fugitives littered their back trail with abandoned food and cooking gear, even a loaded mule, in their haste to reach the

Mexican border. But as the posse closed in, the gang turned on them. In the ensuing firefight, one of the possemen died.

The Tucson *Daily Citizen* reported that the lawmen were ambushed in Skeleton Canyon. Deputy Frank Robson went down "at the first volley," with bullets through his forehead and his temple. The deputy's horse galloped off with him, dead or dying, and the waiting outlaws took not only the animal, but also Robson's money, watch, and revolver.

Leatherwood jumped from his horse as the panicked animal bolted. Lawman Hildreth then killed Black Jack's mount, but the bandit caught the sheriff's horse and managed to switch saddles, only to have the lawman's animal killed before Black Jack could mount.

Hildreth's horse also went down, but Hildreth, wounded, fought on, though the tree behind which he sheltered was filled with lead. Leatherwood, Fly, Alvord, and another posseman named Johnson also fought back as best they could, but they were shooting only at puffs of smoke.

After the firing died away, the battered posse found their quarry vanished. The lawmen followed, reinforced by more possemen, including deadly man hunter Texas John Slaughter ("I say, I say, shoot first and shout 'throw up your hands' after"). According to one version of the tale, Slaughter was not impressed with the posse's actions thus far, and said so: "I say," he commented, "you're a fine bunch of officers. If there was any ambushing to be done, why in the heck didn't *you* do it?" It was a fair question.

Pursuit continued, but Leatherwood wrote from a town in Sonora on August 18 that heavy rains had washed out the gang's trail. Southern Pacific detective and sometime Tombstone lawman Billy Breakenridge reported that the robbers were back in the United States, holed up at the San Simon Cattle Company's horse ranch.

The gang carried on its evil ways, hitting the San Simon railroad station and both the post office and Wickersham's Store at Bowie. In between, they "liberated" horses whenever they needed new mounts, although in most cases they were careful to let the owners know where their stock was ultimately left. It paid to keep good relations with ordinary people when you were on the run: like paying for breakfast at the little Joe Schaefer ranch with a couple of Bull Durham sacks of post office change. That sort of largesse made people feel better disposed toward you, and after all, it's not hard to be generous with somebody else's money.

The frustrated officers kept up the pursuit, and the hunters now included Jeff Milton, the bulldog Wells Fargo man. Along the way he and a deputy stayed a night at Brandt's Store in San Simon. Brandt welcomed them with delight, since he had already been held up once by the High Fives and feared the outlaws would visit him again. And while Milton was at the store, a cowboy came in, bragging about how Christian was making fools of the officers, and how he himself "could run the officers out of the country with a smoking corn cob."

Such boasting was never wise around Jeff Milton. "Go up there," he told the deputy, "and box his jaws. I'll be a-watchin' him, and if he beats you to the draw I'll kill him."

"Sure," said the deputy, "it'll be a pleasure," and whopped the cowboy smartly under Milton's watchful eye. "I didn't see no smoking corn cobs," said Milton afterward.

But the High Fives had now determined to promote themselves to the criminal big time. And so, on a moonless night in October, the gang hit the eastbound Atlantic and Pacific train at the Rio Puerco trestle over in New Mexico. The robbery should have been easy, for the train obligingly stopped while the engineer inspected a faulty piston rod.

The gang threw down on the train crew, shooting the brakeman in the hand when he came forward to see what the trouble was. But these were the High Fives, and now the usual fruits of bad luck and bad planning appeared again, in the form of a train passenger, Deputy US Marshal Horace Loomis.

Loomis guessed something was wrong up front, and so he thoughtfully loaded his shotgun and stepped quietly out into the night. He saw the engineer uncoupling the express car as Code Young shouted orders at him. Without ceremony, the officer dropped Young, who regained his feet and snapped off a couple of rounds from his pistol before the marshal gave him the second barrel. *Exit* Code Young. The rest of the gang, uncertain what had happened to Young, at least realized that something was very wrong, and they galloped off into the night without their loot. Foiled again.

The gang went on with their small-time robberies, holding up a couple of stages and a series of isolated stores. As usual, their labors produced only pittances of money, plus bits and pieces of liquor and tobacco. There was a good deal of casual brutality connected with these robberies: Bob Hayes pistol-whipped one elderly country postmaster, for example, because he objected to giving up $5.50, all the money he had.

There wasn't much profit in robbing isolated stores, like the one in tiny Separ, between Deming and Lordsburg, New Mexico. After that strike, they ran into a posse at the Diamond A horse camp. The story goes that the gang arranged with sympathetic cowboys to display a white cloth on the corral when it was safe to visit the ranch. They hadn't counted on the law moving in and detaining everybody at the camp, spoiling the signal system. And so, when Black Jack and Bob Hayes rode into camp, all unsuspecting, the officers rose up out of their hiding place in a salt lick and blazed away.

They blew Bob Hayes off his horse, quite dead, probably killed by the rifle of town marshal Fred Higgins of Roswell—although another story says he was eliminated at a different time by a Santa Fe conductor somewhere around Kingman, Arizona. Black Jack got away from the Diamond A, even though his horse was shot by the lawmen. The story goes that Christian, single-handed, heaved the dying animal up far enough to pull his Winchester clear, and then shot his way out of

Black Jack Christian WESTERN HISTORY COLLECTIONS, UNIVERSITY OF OKLAHOMA
LIBRARY

the ambush. A posseman had shot five times at the outlaw leader, at a range at which it seemed he could not miss, but Christian escaped unscathed, largely because of the bucking and twisting of his frantic horse.

Milton and the other hunters could not close with the gang. However, in February 1897, a train robbery in New Mexico went sour. Black Jack's own paranoia moved him to kill one Red Sanders, who, he thought, had talked to the law. It was after that stupid and unnecessary murder that Christian moved south, to hide out east of Clifton, Arizona, in a tangled, wild canyon, to this day called Black Jack Canyon. And it was in that desolate place that the tireless law finally caught up with him.

As is common in the mythology of the West, there are a couple of different stories about the end of Black Jack Christian. After the failed attempt on the A&P train at Rio Puerco, the gang hid out at a "goat ranch" near Clifton. There they planned another strike, but before they could do the job, an informer tipped off the law. Deputy Marshal Hall, the formidable Fred Higgins, and possemen Bill Hart, Crook-neck Johnson, and Charlie Paxton set up an ambush in Cole Creek Canyon, down in Graham County.

Ironically, it was a lost hat that put paid to Black Jack's career. Disappointed, the lawmen had already folded up their trailside ambush and were riding toward a ranch to ask for breakfast, when Fred Higgins turned back to look for his hat. It was at this moment that the posse saw three men on the trail behind them, already reaching for their weapons. The first shot came from Higgins, however, whom the outlaws had not seen. The three bandits broke for safety in the thick vegetation, but the posse saw one of them stagger before he reached cover.

The officers, accurately assessing the area as very hostile and very dangerous, decided they had not lost anything in that heavy brush. Instead, they did not try then to search for whomever they had hit, but prudently withdrew to nearby Clifton. Later in the day, however, a cowboy named Bert Farmer passed down the same trail driving horses, and he stopped when the beasts shied at something near the trail.

It was Bill Christian, mortally wounded. He was taken to a nearby ranch, but he did not last long. Dying, he murmured that it didn't matter "who he was, or what his name might be." A Mormon freighter brought into Clifton all that remained of the bold bandit, tossed on top of a load of lumber. A lot of self-appointed experts ran to identify the body, and some of them, inspired either by ignorance or friendship for the deceased, identified the body as outlaw Black Jack Ketchum.

According to Tombstone lawman Billy Breakenridge—one of those who confused Christian with Ketchum—an ambush party led by Deputy Sheriff Ben Clark caught Christian's gang about daylight on April 27, 1897, killing both Black Jack and gang member George Musgrave. Another source differs, and writes that only Christian went down, riddled with four slugs from the weapon of famous man hunter Jeff Milton. Both accounts are probably at least partly wrong.

Musgrave seems to have survived the ambush in which Bill Christian died. And Milton, a very tough Wells Fargo man, was not part of the ambush party that killed Christian. Afterward, however, he ran down other High Fives members, and it was Milton's shotgun that finally did in Three-Fingered Jack Dunlap, veteran of the bungled Nogales raid, and a journeyman villain in his own right.

The two bandits who got away were probably Musgrave and Bob Christian. Christian surfaced in Mexico in the autumn of 1897, was arrested and escaped, then dropped out of sight forever. Musgrave appeared later in Colorado, then got himself arrested in Nebraska in December of 1909. He is said to have lived on in South America, either as businessman or rustler or maybe both, depending on what tales you read. He never returned to the United States, dying probably in 1947.

One curious postscript remains. Ketchum made an intriguing comment in April 1901, on the day he was to be hanged in Clayton, New Mexico. He knew Black Jack Christian, he said, and Christian was still alive: "Oh yes," said Ketchum, "I have an idea where he is but I won't tell."

And he didn't. The secret, if there was one, went to the grave with Ketchum—both parts of him, for the shock of the drop parted him from his head, and he was buried in two pieces.

So passed the High Fives. Considering the amount of time they spent living rough and running from the law, and the nickel-and-dime scores their robberies produced, in the end they were a remarkably unsuccessful gang of outlaws, with little to show for their efforts. Unless you consider the tally of the dead. . . .

CHAPTER 6

Vicious and Inept

The DeAutremonts and the Railroad

Vicious indeed, and that was on their good days. The DeAutremont brothers, Hugh, Ray, and Roy, are in the running for the title of all-time worst scum in the robbery business. They are also among the stupidest, which is saying quite a lot, considering their short career and the host of formidable competitors for the designation.

Born in Iowa and Arkansas, they ended up as West Coast boys. Their father was a barber in Eugene, Oregon, and the elder boys turned their hands to lumberjacking. The two older DeAutremonts, twin brothers Ray and Roy, were twenty-three; Hugh was only nineteen.

When young Hugh graduated from high school in 1923, he joined Ray and Roy out in Silverton, Oregon, where the brothers worked for four months or so until the Big Money beckoned and they embarked on their dubious claim to fame: They decided to hold up Southern Pacific train number 13, the so-called "Gold Special," running between Portland

and San Francisco. Once upon a time, it had in fact regularly carried very large shipments of gold. The brothers thought it still might. Then their little holdup would make them rich, a fine payday for very little work.

It turned out instead to be not only one of the last train holdups on record, but also one of the bloodiest of all time.

At least one brother, Ray, had spent some time as a "Wobblie," a member of the radical and violent International Workers of the World (IWW). His Wobblie membership got him nothing but some reformatory time, which obviously didn't teach him anything, but maybe it did provide a little graduate schooling from the pros.

He made his trip to stir after an Independence Day celebration turned very bad indeed. The city of Centralia, Washington, was having a parade in which the American Legion was proudly marching, and every building in town was flying the Stars and Stripes . . . except the building occupied by the radical International Workers of the World.

It's unclear just what happened next, but it is certain that when the legionnaires reached IWW headquarters, they were stopped, and gunfire erupted almost immediately. Three legionnaires died in the fusillade, and one Wesley Everest ran out the back door of the IWW building only to find the river in his way. He turned and shot down the nearest legionnaire and then inexplicably gave himself up and was promptly taken to jail.

But that night Centralia suffered a total blackout, and when the sun came up the next morning, Wesley was found suspended from a bridge, full of bullets. That made five dead, Wesley and the four legionnaires, and the great state of Washington had had quite enough of the IWW. What followed was a series of mass arrests, and one of those swept up was Ray DeAutremont.

Ray unadvisedly announced that he was proud to be a Wobblie, and while he was in jail, he and another prisoner tried an escape attempt and bungled it. That got him another year behind bars.

That didn't improve his temper once he was released, and so he conspired with twin brother Roy to pick up some easy money by robbing people. That didn't work out either; the brothers' inept planning was already starting to show.

First it was to be a bank, and Ray and Roy watched their target an entire day in a chilly drizzle, which turned into a downpour later. They were still lying in wait, huddled together, when a big Buick pulled up in front of the bank, and a real holdup followed before their very eyes . . . only it was the men in the Buick doing the robbing. Ray was minded to intervene—sort of a "we were here first" notion—until Roy reminded him that their guns were empty.

Next they traveled south, looking for opportunity. They found it, or thought they did, in little Cannon Beach, Oregon. They chose a shop as a target and worked out a plan to rob the owner when he left at the end of the business day with the receipts. Trouble was, they went to sleep in the ditch from which they were going to jump the shop owner and woke only after their target had gone home.

Curses! Foiled again!

There were other problems also impeding their career in crime, among them the fact that neither Ray nor Roy knew how to drive a car. And in this dismal winter of 1922–23, there was little work to be had, which heightened Ray's already well-developed feeling that an oppressive world was against him. Roy worked as a barber, but he had eye trouble and was afraid of going blind.

Somewhere about now the brothers began to talk about a really major crime, and the planning began. In the summer of 1923, little brother Hugh left his mother's home in New Mexico and returned to be with Ray and Roy.

Hugh had done well in high school, both academically and athletically. Still, he fell in with his brothers' planning for the criminal big time. It was to be nothing less than a railway express car, a bonanza that would keep them in deep clover for the rest of their lives. This was perhaps a bit ambitious, since they had so far been a flop at planning even the simplest stickup.

They began by buying a used Nash automobile and adding a pile of ammunition, at least one shotgun, one or more .45 pistols, and some other equipment, including three rucksacks to haul away all that loot. They hit a construction site and stole dynamite, blasting caps and wire, and an exploder.

The next step was to find a safe base of operations, and they made do with an abandoned shack that provided at least some shelter. They passed their days figuring out how to use the dynamite and practicing their marksmanship, until they decided they were at last ready. Almost.

They had the odd notion that the Nash would be dangerous get-away transport, so they added another strange, additional complexity. Hugh would drive their car into Eugene and stash it in their father's garage. Then, *after* the robbery was complete, Hugh would ride the rails back to Eugene, collect the car, and pick up his brothers.

So the grand plan—such as it was—started into action and immediately hit a snag. Actually, it was a cow it hit, an unfortunate animal Hugh managed to run into on his way to Eugene. That stopped the execution of the brothers' plan for a few days, until the car could be repaired.

Meanwhile, Ray and Roy had indulged in some practice boarding a train, in the course of which Roy managed to injure one knee. They did get back to the cabin hideout, and there they had a last-minute conference with Hugh, in the course of which they apparently tried to talk the younger brother out of going along on the robbery. Hugh was determined, however, and so the die was cast.

After all this preparation, the brothers boarded train number 13 near Siskiyou station, not far from the border between California and Oregon. There was a tunnel at that point—also numbered 13—but apparently the brothers were not superstitious enough to make their big score someplace else.

They knew that all trains were required to slow far down and finally to stop just north of the tunnel's mouth to check their brakes before starting the long descent southward. The tunnel would be, they thought, the perfect place for the newly minted DeAutremont gang to attack the train.

The brothers had gone to a great deal of trouble in preparing for their big payday. In addition to marksmanship practice, they had tried out part of their store of the dynamite, too, although they had the misfortune of having no railroad car on which to practice. They had even gone to the trouble of preparing to evade pursuit by obtaining a large quantity of pepper and sacks soaked in creosote to throw off trailing bloodhounds.

They had heard, maybe from an accomplice, that the train was carrying some forty thousand dollars, a substantial sum in the autumn of 1923. And so they had their eyes on number 13's express car; even the greenest train robber knew that's where the money traveled, if there was any on board (ironically, this time there wasn't). But the express agent inside, like so many courageous men in his business, refused to open the car.

The brothers—vicious but not very bright—responded with dynamite, a charge so heavy that it blew out the whole front of the car and set a fire so intense that the robbers could not get in to collect the bonanza they thought was inside. The gutsy agent died, either in the explosion or in the fire, and the brothers had gotten nothing.

Tragically, when the brakeman ran forward toward the fire, thinking the boom had been a boiler explosion on the engine, the DeAutremont boys shot him down; and finally, apparently out of pure meanness, they murdered both the fireman and the engineer while they were standing helplessly with their hands raised.

In a later statement, one brother matter-of-factly admitted they killed at least two of the train crew to prevent possible identification. Maybe the brothers' motive was to eliminate any witnesses against them, maybe it wasn't. But it did something far more dangerous to them; what it certainly did was launch a dogged, relentless pursuit.

The blast had been deliberately set off inside the tunnel to muffle the noise. It didn't. The roar was heard in a Southern Pacific maintenance camp just across the California border.

And so the law gave chase, but they had a lot of ground to make up. The brothers unwittingly helped their pursuers a good deal: They managed to leave lots of evidence behind; the question their pursuers had to solve was what to make of it. There were a couple of backpacks—no need for them, there being no gold to carry, a pistol, the exploder, and a pair of stained coveralls. Without these, the law would almost certainly have come to a dead end; after all, the brothers, save Ray, had no criminal record, and even his connection with real crime was minimal. But the wanton murders changed the situation.

Now forensic analysis was virtually unknown in those distant days, but Edward Heinrich, a chemistry professor at the University of California, did a surprisingly sophisticated analysis of the evidence, and this is what he found: One of the men you're after is a lumberjack, he said; he has Douglas fir needles in the pockets of his overalls, and the position of the pitch stains on the overalls show he is left-handed. A bonus the detectives discovered was a piece of faded paper in one overall pocket. The professor managed to bring out some writing on it, and behold! It turned out to be a registered mail receipt for mail from one brother to another. The lawmen were assembling a fairly clear picture of the robbers.

The pistol's serial number led back to the store whence it came, and there officers found a receipt, with which they traced the Colt back to the buyer. He'd used an alias, but the investigating officers found that the buyer, "William Elliott," was none other than Ray DeAutremont. An express tag further identified the brothers, and the hunt was on.

There was lots of other evidence, too, including Hugh's grandiose *nom de crime*, "J. James," which led investigators to the hotel in which

Hugh had stayed. The Nash also pointed to the brothers (once it had served as evidence it became a police car), and there were also various letters and an insurance policy sent to still another brother.

Meanwhile, the brothers had hidden out in their primitive shack. When the food began to run low, Ray elected to go down to civilization to pick up the Nash and get some news. It was not good. There were wanted posters—complete with pictures—all over Ashland and Medford; he concluded that he could not safely get to Eugene and turned back without the car.

Once he had shared his bad news with his brothers, they elected to leave their hideout and run for it; and so, at the end of October 1923 they set out in miserable winter weather, without proper gear, trying to make it to the coast. They gave that notion up when they saw the extent of the search still under way and instead headed south through driving snow for the California line. In the end they split up, agreeing to meet on New Year's Day five years thence at a YMCA in New York.

They wouldn't make it.

They had about four years of freedom left, with much wandering and nothing of the good life. The railroad detectives in particular stuck to their trail like burrs on a hound's tail. They were not about to give up.

Hugh enlisted in the army under an alias, serving in the Philippines, but even there he was finally run to earth after another soldier noticed that he resembled one of those DeAutremont boys. Hugh was worth a little more than five thousand dollars to his informant, which sure beat corporal's pay. Wanted posters sometimes get wonderful results.

The other two brothers saw a lot of the rest of the United States, including Michigan, Ohio, and West Virginia. But at last the inevitable happened, and a coworker recognized Ray and Roy for who they were. By this time Ray had married and had a child, with a second on the way. It had been a love match, at least for the lady, and so Ray had managed to badly damage some more lives.

In the end the brothers had some luck, more than they deserved. Hugh had long since been tried and convicted, and now Roy and Ray stopped protesting their innocence . . . they had already admitted their identity. The court's sentence for all three was prison for life.

Roy finally drifted off into a land of his own. Episodes of violence in prison finally led to a trip to a mental hospital and a prefrontal lobotomy. The surgery did indeed fix the violent behavior, but it did a good deal more. He spent the rest of his days as a vegetable, finally dying in a nursing home at age eighty-three.

Hugh was finally paroled after thirty-one years in prison; he lived only a few months as a free man before cancer got him. Ray was finally paroled at the age of sixty-one, after serving thirty-four years behind bars. He died in 1984.

It hadn't been much of a life for any of them. For the DeAutremonts, for those who loved them, for the railroad men and their families, it had all been a terrible waste, as badly bungled a criminal enterprise as any in history.

They had at least set a sort of criminal record.

CHAPTER 7

The Wrong Town

The McCarty Clan at Delta

"Murder!" screamed the headline of the Delta, Colorado, *Independent*. "Three Robbers Commit a Horrible Deed." The *Independent*, a little weekly, devoted the whole front page and two columns of three more pages to the details of this local excitement. The sensation scarcely left space for the usual advertisements, among which was some hype for a medication called *Ripans Tabules*, which apparently cured everything, or for Gale Bros., sort of a one-stop shopping center. The Gale boys were purveyors of furniture and carpets, did some contracting and mill work, and were undertakers and embalmers besides. They would have lots of work this day.

For dead on the floor of Delta's little Farmer's and Merchant's Bank was an unarmed bank cashier, father of a large family, a bullet through his skull. Two more men, both bandits, sprawled in their own blood on a Delta street, and a grim posse was in hot pursuit of one surviving outlaw.

In the autumn of 1893, Delta was a quiet little town, very much like hundreds of other young, growing communities across the West. It had been called Uncompahgre not long before, but it was platted in the spring of 1882 as Delta, named for its nearness to the delta of the Gunnison and Uncompahgre Rivers. And Delta was vigorous and growing: In 1883, Delta had already boasted two saloons, three hardware stores, three lawyers, a couple of dozen other commercial enterprises, and two banks.

September 7 was a miserably hot day, unfit for man or beast. A Delta resident of the time called it "stifling," the sort of day on which people move very slowly and stay in the shade if they have no pressing business out under the blazing sun. Nobody in Delta was interested in excitement on a day like that, but excitement was on the way, the sort of excitement nobody wanted, in Delta or anyplace else.

Delta's little Farmer's and Merchant's Bank was about to receive an unwelcome visit. Veteran outlaw Tom McCarty had his eye on the citizens' hard-earned savings, and with him were his brother Bill and Bill's seventeen-year-old son Fred. The three had been watching the little town and its bank for several days, and on this oppressive seventh of September they were at last ready to move.

Tom McCarty was a professional hoodlum. His father may have been William, once a surgeon with Tennessee Confederate troops, or maybe one Alexander, nicknamed "Doc." Whoever he was, he brought his large family west to Montana and then to Utah, where they settled for a while close to Circleville, home of one Leroy Parker, better known as Butch Cassidy.

The family kept moving, on to Nevada, then back to Utah in 1877. Tom and Bill ranched together for a while, and they did well enough to sell out at a good profit in 1884. One story says Tom managed to gamble away his share, whereat he betook himself to a new career in outlawry, rustling, robbing, and shooting at least one man.

Bill is said to have gone off to Missouri, where, an unlikely legend has it, he rode either with Jesse James or with Cole Younger. A neat trick that, since by 1884 Jesse was permanently dead and Cole was doing hard time in Minnesota's Stillwater Prison. Whatever nefarious doings he may or may not have been up to in Missouri, Bill married (for the second time, without benefit of a divorce) and shot a man "over robbery loot," which peccadillo got him a term in prison.

Tom rode with Butch Cassidy and Matt Warner, among others, and had been part of the famous 1893 robbery of the San Miguel bank of Telluride, Colorado. That raid, which netted more than twenty thousand dollars, was reputed to be Cassidy's first venture into bank robbery. Tom is also a central figure in the celebrated robbery of the First National Bank of Denver in the spring of 1889.

The story goes that McCarty made an appointment with bank president David Moffat and showed the banker a bottle of clear liquid. "It's nitroglycerine," said McCarty, and he demanded the banker write him a check for twenty-one thousand dollars and cash it. McCarty slipped his loot to a confederate outside the bank and returned to his hotel, where he disposed of his bottle of water.

McCarty and career-outlaw Matt Warner robbed a gambling hall in Butte, Montana, and sought shelter at a hardscrabble "ranch" in Baker, Oregon, owned by McCarty's brother Bill, now out of prison. Things were tough in the ranching business for Bill and his son Fred, and both joined Tom to follow the apparently easy money of the owl-hoot trail. It would prove to be an exceedingly poor decision in the long run, however short the grass was at Baker.

For a while, however, the outlaw business went fairly smoothly. The four men robbed a placer camp called Sparta, in Oregon, coming away with a haul of currency and gold nuggets. They rode into Moscow, Idaho, to rob, of all things, a circus, and then returned to Enterprise, Oregon, to rob a bank. More holdups followed, including a bank in Roslyn, Washington.

The Roslyn job went bad: Tom shot a man in the stomach and the gang had to run for it, with a posse hot on their heels. Warner was eventually captured and spent some time in jail awaiting trial. Acquitted and released, he was smart enough to quit once he got out of jail. McCarty wasn't that bright.

Now without the redoubtable Warner, and just a few weeks after his trial, the McCarty brothers and young Fred were determined to empty the coffers of the Farmer's and Merchant's, one of Delta's two banks. The story of what happened when they tried to do so varies depending on who is telling it. A couple of versions of the raid don't even agree on the date: While it is clear that the holdup took place on September 7, other accounts have it happening on September 3 or 27.

The three outlaws apparently arrived at Delta about the first of the month and took some time casing the town. They seem to have spent considerable time in the Steve Bailey Saloon, otherwise known as the Palace Sampling Rooms, conveniently placed right across the street from the bank. They camped outside the town prior to the raid, perhaps in nearby Escalante Canyon—at least they are thought to have stopped there for a meal at the John Musser cattle ranch. They brought with them a string of spare mounts, and they took their time about sizing up the bank and the town.

When in town, the outlaws stabled their horses at Fadely's corral on the north side of Delta, and they spent some time yarning with one George Smith, keeper of the steam engine that drove the municipal water pump. The three hoodlums were chatty types, asking what were later called "innocent-sounding questions" over a friendly drink in one of the town's watering holes.

In the afternoons they rode out of town, letting it be known that they were shopping around for a ranch site. One source says young Fred was used as a scout for the gang, and he even got involved in a marble game with some of the Delta boys. The outlaws ate a meal at a restaurant called "Bricktop's" on Main Street, and at least two more at Central House. In between a drink or two and some card playing at Steve Bailey's, they shopped for shoes and a bottle of whiskey.

On the seventh of September, they were ready. Tom probably performed his usual role: He liked to be the outside man, watching the street and holding the horses for the other two robbers. A local citizen watched Tom down at least one slug of Dutch courage just before he entered the alley behind the bank with all three men's horses. At about quarter after ten, Bill and his son walked into the bank. It probably did not occur to any of the outlaws that this broiling day was the anniversary of the James-Younger gang's disaster at Northfield in 1876.

Inside the bank were two men: cashier A. T. Blachley, as the local paper named him (or Blachly or Blachey, depending on which other sources you read), and H. H. Wolbert, teller and assistant cashier. One book on the Wild Bunch puts a third employee in the bank, a bookkeeper called John Trew, but no other authority does. At the back of the bank, in a sort of lean-to he used as an office, sat attorney W. R. Robinson.

Across the street, in Simpson and Corbin's Hardware store—or Simpson and Son's, again depending on the source—sat William Ray Simpson. Simpson—people in Delta called him Ray—was Kentucky born and raised and had moved west with his parents for his health. He settled in Delta but took time out to return to Kentucky for his light of love, Mary Ann Hays.

The pair eloped, the story goes, since Mary Ann's father insisted that his family was superior to any other. Apparently the attraction between the two young people was of some years' standing, for the story goes that Simpson had seen young Mary Ann jumping horses at the county fair back in Kentucky. "There's a pair of thoroughbreds if I've ever seen one," he said, "and I'm going to marry that girl when she grows up."

It's a nice story, maybe even true, and it is certain that Simpson and the lady married—probably on the way west in Decatur, Texas. They settled in Delta and produced three daughters. Simpson was a solid citizen, a respected merchant; he was about to become the town's hero.

To this day there is no certainty about everything that happened inside the bank. Blachley, one of the founders of the bank, was typing; Wolbert was working nearby, and the bank's safe stood wide open. Two men walked into the bank and Blachley got up to wait on them. He found himself looking into the business end of two guns. The bandits demanded the bank's assets forthwith, and one of the robbers, probably young Fred, jumped up on the bank's counter.

Wolbert made a motion toward a pistol but gave it up when one of the bandits warned him against such a rash move. Cashier Blachley, with more courage than discretion, seems to have shouted for help, and one of the outlaws told him to shut up or get his head blown off. Nothing daunted, the gutty cashier shouted again.

This time he got two bullets at close range: The slugs entered his neck and tore out through the top of his head, or maybe—in other versions—he was killed by a single round through the top of the skull. In either case, Blachley's gallant defiance had cost him his life. The Grand Junction *News* also reported, probably erroneously, that the robbers had shot at Wolbert but missed him. At least by now, even if nobody had heard the cashier's call for help, the gunfire told everybody in town there was big trouble at the bank.

Tom McCarty's "autobiography" simply says that two men entered the bank and a third waited outside with the horses, without naming who did what. He also says that the cashier "reached for a pistol" and was shot down. This version is unsupported by any other rendition of the raid, and it sounds very like an after-the-fact attempt to justify cold-blooded murder.

The inside men—probably Bill and Fred McCarty—grabbed a bag of gold coin, snatched handfuls of bills and stuffed them inside their shirts—something between seven hundred and a thousand dollars—then ran out through the lawyer's lean-to at the back of the bank. One version of the story says Tom McCarty "covered the lawyer at his desk," while the other two bandits were busy in the bank, although this seems at odds with Tom's usual job as outside man. Still another account has Tom killing the cashier, after which "Fred rushed to the horses, quickly followed by the other two."

In his book *Desperate Men,* James D. Horan names Tom as the killer, but he also has Matt Warner—who wasn't there—holding the gang's horses. In still another account, "Bill McCarty began scooping money in a bag, Tom leaped over the railing and pushed a six-gun into Blachey's [*sic*] ribs." Fred, in this version, is the man who covered the attorney at the rear of the bank.

Who shot the cashier is not clear, and Horan's account loses some force by claiming erroneously that Blachley's "assistant"—presumably Wolbert—was wounded. Still another version says flatly that young Fred murdered the cashier.

Whatever had happened inside, the robbers dashed into the alley, herding Wolbert along with them, one of the bandits calling to his confederates, "Get on your horses quick, for God's sake." It was good advice, for citizens were already moving toward the front of the bank. One account of the raid says the two inside men got to the alley to find their horses waiting, "but Tom had jumped on his horse and was long gone."

Leaving behind their bag of gold, the outlaws mounted and fled. While Blachley's shouts had apparently not been heard outside the bank because of a high wind, the shots that killed him certainly had been; among those who heard them was Ray Simpson, and he reacted immediately.

According to one version of the Delta raid, he was cleaning his rifle—most accounts call it a .44 Sharps—in the back room of the hardware store, right across Main Street from the bank. Or maybe, according to another version, he just grabbed a repeating rifle from the rack in the store: That rifle would probably have been new stock, and therefore not a Sharps, since the Sharps company had failed in 1881. Other accounts refer to Simpson's "trusty Winchester." The Delta Historical Society reports, however, that it has the very rifle in its museum: a single-shot .40-caliber Sharps.

Simpson himself told a fascinating story about being prepared to take on the robbers. He had, he said later, dreamed that a local bad man had vandalized his shop and he, Simpson, had to shoot the intruder. The vision so stuck in Simpson's mind that next morning he cleaned his rifle—left uncleaned after target practice the day before—and "set it with the cartridges where I could get it quick." In fact, he was telling his father and the town night watchman of his strange dream when two shots rang out in the bank across the street.

Although angry citizens were gathering in front of the bank, Simpson noticed that there were no horses tethered there and guessed the gang had stashed their mounts in the alley behind the bank. Simpson ran out on the street, hearing somebody yell, "get your gun; it's a holdup." He sprinted to the corner of Third Street and Main, loading the single-shot Sharps as he went. At the corner Simpson turned toward the alley as the three outlaws galloped past him.

As the three McCartys galloped away from the bank, Simpson raised the Sharps and pulled down on the nearest one. He hit Bill in the back of the head—"in the hatband" according to an article in the *Independent*—and the bullet tore off the top of Bill's head complete with hat. One account says Bill's few brains ended up twenty feet away from the rest of him. Fred hesitated—Horan even says Fred "returned to kneel" over his father—but this sounds a bit like journalistic embroidery, since a glance would have told Fred that the top of Bill's head was not where it used to be.

Simpson said that Fred fired three times at him and paused only long enough to glance at his father, quickly perceiving that the older man was dead. A later article in the local paper has Fred galloping back to his fallen father, "coming to a skidding halt," and leaning over to look at the lifeless body on the ground.

Whatever Fred did, it was the last thing he did, for Ray Simpson put the next round into the base of Fred's skull. (One sensational account says Simpson's bullet "split his heart.") A citizen named John Travis reportedly fired several shots at the bandits with a revolver. He doesn't seem to have hit any of the outlaws, but it may have been one of his bullets that in fact killed Bill's unfortunate horse.

Simpson had done some fine shooting, for by the time he fired at Fred McCarty, Simpson may have been as much as a block away from the fleeing bandits. Fred's corpse stayed in the saddle for another block, his horse galloping on, and there the second McCarty bit the dust. Loose currency was scattered up and down the alley. Asked about his marksmanship later, Simpson commented that where he came from, Kentucky, "Boys are taught to shoot squirrels in the head to keep from spoiling the meat."

The usual moonshine surrounds the Delta robbery. Along with the "trusty Winchester" references, there is a nonsensical story that has Simpson shooting Bill McCarty "from the hip" and refers to Fred as Bill's "nephew." The reference to Fred and the marble game also seems a little hard to swallow, for kids grew up fast in those faraway days, and it's hard to imagine an experienced outlaw hunkered down in the dust with a couple of the local urchins. And no experienced marksman shoots anybody "from the hip," except in Hollywood.

Along the way Simpson—or somebody—shot one of the outlaws' horses, an animal that a local citizen saw "sprawled in the alley against the door-sill of the store," maybe the hardware emporium run by Simpson and his father. It was probably Bill's horse, which may have galloped back toward the bank after its rider was killed. The horse may have been mortally wounded by the bullet that killed its rider, and so Simpson believed. Or, maybe, according to *The Wild Bunch at Robber's*

Roost, some unidentified "smart aleck" shot the animal. In any case, this horse trotted on down to the post office hitching rack and stood among other horses until it bled to death. Fred's mount, dripping with its rider's blood, was caught by a local lady.

Tom, veteran outlaw, wanted nothing more to do with that deadly rifle, even if he did leave two kinsmen dead in the street behind him. He "let it be known later, however, that the two or three bullets Simpson sent in his direction came uncomfortably close." He realized the gang had been well and truly whipped by a single man, and he did not stay upon the order of his going.

He changed horses in the gang's camp outside town and lit out at the high lope for southwestern Colorado. He left behind several horses and a mule, and, as it turned out, he also left the bank-robbing business for good.

A manuscript that purports to be McCarty's autobiography was sent to his father-in-law and supposedly published by a newspaper in Manti, Utah. It is now in the possession of the Utah State Historical Society. Charles Kelly, who wrote of the Wild Bunch, believed the manuscript to be genuine. In it, McCarty tells his own story of the fight at Delta. Here he describes the story of the gang's flight:

> *As we passed the first street I heard the sharp crack of a rifle, and looking for my partners, I saw one of them [Bill] fall from his horse; my other companion [Fred] being a little ahead, then partly turned his horse as though he wanted to see where the shot came from. I told him quickly to go on, but as I spoke another shot came which struck his horse and before he could get his animal in motion another shot came which struck him and he fell dead. His horse began to run back toward the place where the shots had come from . . . looking back I saw a man standing by the corner of a building, having what I supposed was a Winchester and shooting as fast as possible at me. . . . The first man he killed could not have been more than*

twenty-five yards from him . . .; the other about one hundred and
fifty feet . . . several bullets passed so near me that I felt the force of
the balls as they passed; one of his bullets struck my horse . . . near
the heel, which crippled him.

[A]fter I had traveled about seventy-five miles I found some
friends who told me that both of my relatives had been shot dead,
both having received the bullets through the head. . . .

After the raid there was some debate about the real identity of
the dead outlaws. Some said they were obviously McCartys; others
disagreed. At first, it was thought that the older of the two dead
bandits was Tom McCarty, not his brother. It did not take long to
resolve the puzzle once men who actually knew the family saw the
corpses.

Delta sheriff Giradet raised a posse—which included the redoubtable Simpson—and gave chase, but could not come up with fleeing Tom
McCarty. They recovered his horse, cut up, saddle sore, and exhausted,
but McCarty had changed mounts. The posse at last returned on September 12, their only reward a couple of McCarty's other horses and
an abandoned pack. They had come close enough to the outlaw to find
a campfire still burning, but they never saw the man himself.

The remains of his confederates were hauled off to Gale Brothers
Undertaking Parlor. There, after they had set a while, both corpses
were propped up to have their picture taken, after the fashion of the
times. The photographer's son, young Ben Laycock, about ten years old
according to the Delta Historical Society, had been "bathing prints" in
front of his father's shop when the fireworks began.

Now—or the next day according to an interview with Ben many
years later—young Ben helped out with the arrangements to photograph the bodies. Undertaker Gale, who also dealt in lumber and furniture, helped to prop up the remains. Fred was stiff enough to stand
up on his own, but Bill kept sagging inconveniently. So Gale borrowed

some boards from the lumberyard and propped Bill into a suitable upright position.

They put Bill's hat on him to decently cover the spot where Simpson's bullet had removed part of his head, and he stayed upright long enough for young Ben's brother to take his photo. Bill sagged and collapsed again after the picture was taken, but by then he was superfluous, and nobody cared.

In later years, Ben may have embroidered a little on the tale of the photos. "The old man," he wrote, meaning Bill, was "limp as a wet sack," so Ben and Gale had to hold him up for his last picture. The rest of Ben's story is worth quoting:

> *Finally we put boards under his arms, and Gale and I held him until just as Henry was ready to take the picture. He looked like hell with the whole top of his head shot off, so Gale rustled around and got a hat to set on his head. We let go of him, jumped back out of the way, Henry snapped the picture, and we grabbed him before he toppled over on the ground.*

Well, maybe, but considering the length of time it took to make a decent exposure in those days, it may be that Ben was exaggerating just a mite. It's a good story, anyway.

Having done their duty for the camera, Bill and Fred were carted off to Potter's Field and planted in a single box, apparently without ceremony. The *Delta Independent* says they were dug up the following Sunday—twice—to be identified, then reinterred. In the miserable heat of the time, no doubt some haste in burial—and reburial—was deemed appropriate. Another account tells us that Bill's uncle-by-marriage came from Moab, Utah, and a police officer came from Denver, to identify the remains of the two bandits.

A vest found on one of the horses yielded an interesting insight into outlaw bookkeeping. The *Delta Independent* reported discovery of a notebook listing various purchases, "largely whiskey," the prices added together and divided by three: "My part" read a notation next to the result. Other notes listed the writer's gambling losses, presumably to his companions, showing the "grand total I owe $493.00."

Simpson's heroics came too late for Blachley. Wolbert, shaken but unhurt, had the miserable task of telling Mrs. Blachley that her husband had been murdered. Blachley's funeral was attended by several hundred people, the largest crowd ever to turn out for a burying in Delta. The paper carried a fine eulogy by a local lady, which concluded,

And all who mourn their dead today
Look on the bright and changing earth
And see in shelter of decay,
The symbol of immortal birth.

The widow was left with nine sons, whom she raised on a "poor, barren, little ranch." The gallant lady was an Oberlin College graduate—quite a rarity on the frontier in those days—and supported her family by teaching music. It is pleasant to note that her boys went on to be prominent, educated men.

After the Delta disaster Tom McCarty dropped out of sight. He is said to have "returned to his old hideout in the Blue Mountains to quiet his shattered nerves" and brood upon the repulse of his last raid. Maybe so. He had, after all, lost two kinsmen to a single rifleman, and had taken to his heels in flight. His ignominious retreat could not have fit his own image of himself. In any case, his sulking is supposed to have given rise to one of the most colorful tales in the history of American outlawry. It goes like this.

In the fall of 1896, the story goes, Tom McCarty sent word to Simpson, by then Delta's postmaster, that he was going to kill him. Just how the message was sent not every version of the tale recounts.

One source says McCarty came to Delta and sent "an emissary"—not further identified—to tell Simpson he was doomed.

The tale of Ray Simpson's answer was classic. He sent McCarty—by emissary or otherwise—a small card punched with ten bullet holes, put there by Simpson "at 225 feet" "with his new Winchester." Another version of the story, recounted in *The Outlaw Trail*, tells that after Simpson received the threat from McCarty "a government detective was sent to trap the outlaw if possible." It continues: "To this operative Simpson presented his famous card, with instructions to deliver it to McCarty at the earliest opportunity. It consisted of a small piece of black cardboard perforated with ten holes, all within the circumference of half a dollar."

At 225 feet? Some shooting, that, extraordinary even with a modern rifle and first-class optical sights. This version of the tale also does not explain how the detective was supposed to make delivery.

Still another account—by a Delta resident—tells the reader that Simpson received threatening letters for years after the raid, that Mrs. Simpson "suffered a complete nervous breakdown" and died when the couple's youngest daughter was very small. Another version of the raid does not mention the famous card at all, but it does repeat the story that in later years Simpson received threatening letters, apparently from McCarty. This account says Simpson was finally forced to leave Delta and settle in California. He is said to be buried in Glendale.

The story of the perforated card appeared in the *Salt Lake City Herald* in January 1897. Police officers in Utah, said the paper, "are inclined to the opinion that McCarty does not possess his old-time spirit and will therefore never seek to molest the redoubtable Colorado postmaster." That he did not, whether from native caution, the threat of the card, or because the whole thing never happened at all, we'll never know for sure.

Considerable uncertainty surrounds Tom McCarty's later years. Variously, he was shot to death about 1900 up in Montana's Bitterroot country after he picked a fight with the wrong man; he was killed near Green River, Utah; he died at Skagway, Alaska, during the gold rush; or he died in California, where he lived with his son Lew. One account has him living peacefully in Wallowa County, Oregon, after the turn of the century, even becoming a justice of the peace and "road supervisor," whatever that may be; others speculate that he fled to South America; or he settled in Oregon and raised a family there.

However Tom McCarty ended his days, he must have been forever haunted by that hot day in Colorado, the day he ran from a single citizen, leaving his kinsmen dead in the dust behind him.

CHAPTER 8

Pioneers

The Reno Boys and the Sport of Train Robbery

You read a lot about the James boys, veterans of countless bad movies, potboilers, and tales of greater or lesser accuracy . . . mostly lesser. Even some of the good writing about the James gang attributes to them the beginning of the fine art of train robbery, presumably because of their several robberies of the iron horse when the gang was at its short-lived zenith.

Not so. That dubious distinction belongs to a much-less-well-known outlaw band called the Reno brothers, who don't get the dubious credit they deserve.

The Renos had their heyday, if that's the word, just after the close of the Civil War. They came from a family of farmers living near Seymour, Indiana, but by the autumn of 1865, John, Simeon, Bill, and Frank Reno had decided that a career in crime was for them. Whether they were moved by some notion of romance and high adventure, simple avarice, or just an allergy to work is unclear.

Whatever motivated the brothers, they started with a bang, but with the career criminal's usual intellectual density, they also started very close to home. For openers, in early 1866, they robbed the treasury of Clinton County. That got Frank arrested, but he was later acquitted, freeing him up to join his siblings in what is almost surely the first American train robbery.

Simeon, John, and a confederate slugged the guard on an Ohio and Mississippi train just after it left the depot at—of all places—Seymour, and down the line a few miles they shoved two safes from the express car. The rest of the boys were waiting and lustily attacked the safes. One they cracked, winning fifteen thousand dollars; the one they couldn't contained about twice as much. Still, it was a good beginning, back when a dollar was a dollar, and it whetted the brothers' appetite for more adventures.

But now they had to cope with the Pinkerton Agency, which had contracted with the express company owning the safes and responsible for their contents. Pinkerton agents drifted into Seymour and tried to establish friendly relations with the Reno boys. They were apparently suspects from the beginning, probably because of Frank's recent criminal history.

All unaware, the brothers continued their newfound career, hitting yet another county treasury, this time in Gallatin, Missouri; that got them another twenty-two thousand dollars, and the stealing business began to look better and better. Then they hit a major snag: The Pinkerton men, reluctant to start a gun battle in Seymour, hit upon a simple, foolproof arrest plan. Running a special train into Seymour, they managed to inveigle John Reno out onto the platform, and there they simply snatched him, without the slightest pretence of due process of law, or even a by-your-leave.

The train immediately carried the kidnappers and their prey away; the rest of the brothers chased the train after they learned of John Reno's misfortune, but they couldn't catch up with the iron horse,

presumably faster than ordinary horseflesh. John was quickly convicted and shipped off to the state pen. If that sounds impossible in
this day of complex criminal litigation and constitutional protections,
it probably is, particularly since the whole business started with a kid-
napping of the defendant. Back then, however, it worked.

Frank Reno now ascended to the purple, as the saying went,
in his brother's place, and under his command the gang went on a
series of successful operations, including the robbery of still another
county treasury, this time in Magnolia, Iowa. The take there was
about fourteen thousand dollars, but the gang left tracks this time.
For in Council Bluffs, Iowa, the Pinkertons found that a citizen
named Rogers, described as an "upstanding resident," in fact had
been a criminal and often went to a saloon run by a onetime coun-
terfeiter. And so when Frank Reno was spotted entering Rogers'
house, a police raid followed, sweeping up Frank, Rogers, and two
counterfeiters.

All four accordingly went off to jail in Council Bluffs, but this time
they managed to escape; it being the first of April, they wrote a large
"April Fool" on the wall of the place before they departed.

So Frank, Simeon, and Bill were together once more, and they
planned a truly spectacular strike. It was to be a train again, this time
on the Ohio and Mississippi Valley line just a few miles away from
Seymour, and it would be spectacular by any measure.

For this job the Reno boys had brought along lots of help, a couple of dozen hard cases. Although the brothers again shortsightedly
staged the holdup just thirteen miles from Seymour, they came away
with a take worth almost one hundred thousand dollars in money and
other valuables.

The Pinkertons of course pursued, and within just four days they
managed to collar three of the desperadoes. But at this point fate
intervened in the form of a local vigilante group, which overpowered
the Pinkerton men in charge of the three and promptly hanged their

charges. There wasn't much due process of law involved this time either, but at least the three wouldn't rob anybody ever again.

Bill and Simeon Reno were luckier. Arrested in July in Indiana, they languished in jail awaiting trial, while the Pinkertons followed Frank and two lesser lights into Canada. They arrested them there, or somehow got them arrested, and began the long, involved process of extradition. Twice while they waited, other criminals unsuccessfully tried to murder agency founder William Pinkerton.

But finally in early October, the glacial legal process ground to completion, and the gang members were moved south to New Albany, Indiana, where they held a sort of reunion with Simeon and Bill. If it was a happy occasion, the good cheer didn't last, for a vigilante band again entered the jail and applied their own idea of due process.

They lynched them all.

CHAPTER 9

Like Father, Like Son

The Clements Family

The given name of both father and son was Emmanuel, but there ended any resemblance to things heavenly. The father, generally known as Mannen, was raised on a ranch in a Texas backwater called, of all things, Smiley. Mannen early on showed an inclination to wander from the straight and narrow path of righteousness; he was suspected of rustling and other minor peccadilloes before he branched out to jail breaking in 1872.

The man he freed was, if anything, a worse thug than he was, none other than John Wesley Hardin, killer of at least twenty-one men; he said it was forty, and it may even have been more. That is, until he was ultimately ushered out of this vale of tears in El Paso by old John Selman. Hardin was Mannen's cousin, and Clements got him out of jail even though Hardin had fought with the Taylor clan against the

Manning Clements

Mannen Clements WESTERN HISTORY COLLECTIONS, UNIVERSITY OF OKLAHOMA
LIBRARY

Taylor family, related to the Clements. In the tangled world of Texas feuds such entanglements were not unknown.

Mannen went on to prosper in the family cattle business, driving herds northward to the Kansas cow towns—with some time out along the way in jail, where his cellmates were John Ringo, Hardin, and one of the Taylor clan. That didn't stop him from running for the office of sheriff; after all, in his part of the world nobody wanted a shrinking violet to maintain the peace.

Mannen met his end—well deserved—in Ballinger, Texas, in 1887 at the hands of Marshal Joe Townsend. Runnels County had been recently created, and Mannen's candidacy for sheriff was opposed. Mannen was having a few in the Senate Saloon when Townsend came in, and some hard words followed. The last one was Townsend's.

But families like the Clements didn't vanish into the musty halls of history that easily.

Mannen's worthy successor was his son, also called Emmanuel, but locally referred to as Mannie. In the 1890s, Mannie teamed up with his vicious cousin John Wesley Hardin and another equally vile relative, this time an in-law, Jim Miller.

Now Hardin is well known in the annals of the murdering business; his uncivilized nature was surely not due to a neglected childhood—one of the standard excuses for growing up mean—for his father was a preacher, and the Hardin family had been prominent in the history of the Texas Republic.

Sadly, whatever fine genes his relatives may have had, Hardin didn't get any. He started turning bad at the tender age of eleven, when he stabbed another boy. He killed his first man at age fifteen. Once he reached a sort of adulthood, Hardin kept on killing here and there, at one point hiding out with his relatives, the Clements boys.

Along the way he rode with his cousins in the bloody Sutton-Taylor feud. He was (for him) relatively quiet for a time, but in 1874 he killed a deputy sheriff, and the long-suffering state of Texas slapped a fourteen-thousand-dollar dead-or-alive reward offer on him, a considerable amount of money for the time.

He fled to Florida with his family, engaging in more or less peaceful pursuits, but in time the Texas Rangers found him even there. And so Hardin finally spent some time in a Texas prison for murder. He studied law while he was behind bars—there went another of the hackneyed excuses for outlawry . . . poor thing, he was just too stupid to get along in the world. He had married along the way, but his wife died while he was in prison, leaving him with three children.

After being paroled, he actually practiced law in Texas for a while, first in Gonzales and later in Junction. There he married again, a much younger woman who, it is said, had the good sense to leave him on their wedding day.

Hardin at last ended up in El Paso, where he spent much of his time with some kindred spirits, of which there was no shortage in the booming, violent border town. Along the way he had words with the Selmans, father and son, men as violent as Hardin was. In fact, he threatened to kill both father and son. Trouble was, the Selmans were the law in El Paso, and they were not inclined to suffer insulting hoodlums gladly.

Nor were they inclined to let chivalry get in the way of satisfaction. And so, while Hardin was shooting dice at the bar in a local saloon, Selman senior walked in behind him. Hardin was obviously having a good time, having just remarked to his companion, a grocer named Brown, "you have four sixes to beat."

Brown didn't have to beat anything, for about then Selman shot Hardin in the back of the head and then pumped two more rounds into him as he lay on the floor. So much for the Hollywood notion of the Code of the West. The Code of the Gunfighter worked infinitely better: no confrontations; no unnecessary risks; after all, if you took such chances, you might get hurt. Shoot 'em in the back if possible; in the back in the dark is even better.

If Hardin was a thoroughly evil man, shirttail relative Jim Miller may have been even worse, far worse. For Miller was an assassin by trade. It was his profession and probably his pleasure. If the money was right, he'd take out just about anybody; his long list of victims even included the formidable Pat Garrett—shot in the back, of course. Miller customarily dressed in funereal black suits and had considerable association with local churches when he wasn't out killing people; hence his nickname, "Deacon Jim."

Less flatteringly, he was also known as "killin' Jim." He seems to have sported an additional clothing item not customarily found on men of the cloth: a steel vest worn under his shirt, a thoughtful accoutrement that saved his life at least once.

For all his pretended piety and his long success at his trade, Miller was betrayed by his own arrogance and overconfidence. Having killed a man named Bobbitt, a leading citizen of Ada, Oklahoma, he made the simpleminded mistake of answering a wire calling him back from safety in Texas. Jim thought it was from the men who had hired him to do the murder in Ada, but it wasn't. Though the names on it were indeed those of the men with whom he had contracted for Bobbitt's murder, the wire was sent by the law.

And so he found himself in the Ada jail with his employers. Arrogant and boastful as ever, he ostentatiously feasted on steak sent in from the local restaurant and announced his intention to hire ace attorney Moman Pruiett for his defense. That proved to be his undoing.

For Pruiett had a phenomenal win record, a product of his great ability and, some said, a well-developed talent for trial rigging. One tale, perhaps apocryphal, tells that when one client retained him by wire, Pruiett responded that he was coming by the next train and bringing "eye-witnesses" with him. Pruiett denied the story the rest of his life, but the legend lives on.

News that the great Pruiett was on the way to defend the odious Miller was the last straw for the long-suffering people of Ada.

Deacon Jim Miller and friends WESTERN HISTORY COLLECTIONS, UNIVERSITY OF
OKLAHOMA LIBRARY

Outraged at the thought that Miller might escape retribution for killing one of their citizens, they took immediate hands-on action.

So Deacon Jim found himself involuntarily broken out of jail
along with his erstwhile employers, dragged to a nearby stable, and
strung up, ad hoc, from a rafter. Jim bragged to the last; he wanted
everybody to remember that he'd killed fifty-one men. Maybe he even
had; it didn't do him any good.

The good people of Ada rejoiced. The local paper commented that
while lynching was ordinarily a bad thing, this one would be approved
by "God and man." If the assumption that the Almighty was on the
side of the citizens was a mite presumptuous, the hanging sure played
well in Ada.

And so passed another minion of the Clements clan.

His in-law Mannie Clements was not an unalloyed success as a bad man, though it wasn't for lack of trying. He left his part of Texas when he fouled up an assassination assignment, the murder for hire of a hoodlum named Pink Taylor. He indeed took a whack at Taylor through an open window, but his shooting was lousy. He missed and killed somebody else. That made him unpopular enough that he felt a pressing need to try out new climes, in this case El Paso.

There, Mannie acquired a star, serving as a deputy sheriff and deputy constable. Now El Paso at the close of the nineteenth century was as tough a town as there ever was in the West, which is saying quite a lot. Mannie seems to have thrived on trouble, and he even got himself arrested for armed robbery in 1908. He went free, however, and the story goes that the jury cared a trifle more about their skins than about law enforcement. One healthy effect his arrest had: His career as a lawman was finished for good.

But as time wore on, Mannie turned more and more to John Barleycorn for solace and to smuggling for income. The commodity he ran across the border into the United States was, however, human. The early twentieth century saw a thriving business in running Chinese illegal immigrants from Mexico into the United States.

However good Mannie's cash flow was from this dirty trade, in the end it proved a bad idea. It got him killed in 1908. In the Coney Island Saloon in El Paso, Mannie got into some sort of dispute with the bartender, one Joe Brown, who apparently was a competitor in the people-smuggling business. Things escalated until the two rivals went for their guns.

Mannie came in second. Like his father, he died on a dirty saloon floor.

CHAPTER 10

Mama's Boys

The Barker Gang and Friends

There is no more bizarre tale in the annals of crime than the story of the Barker gang. Part of it is real, part of it is modern myth, and much of it is overdramatization by journalists writing for a public hungry for anything that could help it forget the dismal days of the Great Depression. All of it is ugly.

The gang was not the monolithic crime machine it is at times portrayed as. Individual members sometimes operated alone or with other career crooks, such as Alvin "Creepy" Karpis, Ray Terrill, and the murderous Larry DeVol. But . . . they were in part a family unit, which made them good newspaper copy, and best of all their guiding light was a woman . . . and not only a woman, but their mother—according to journalistic myth and J. Edgar Hoover, that is.

The fable took root and flourished that "Ma" Barker, as she was inevitably called, was the gang's planner and organizer, and in fact fought beside her boys. It's a fascinating idea, but the truth seems to have been far more prosaic. Still, her fanciful reputation as gang leader and planner refuses to die, in part due to the Barkers' archnemesis, J. Edgar Hoover.

Ma was born in Missouri back in 1873 and christened Arizona Donnie Clark; called Arrie or Kate and still in her teens, she married George Barker and began to give birth to the string of hoodlums who went down in criminal history as the Barker gang. There were four of them: Herman (known as Slim), Fred (called Shorty), Arthur (Doc or Dock), and Lloyd (nicknamed Red). As old-time poker players might have put it, the brothers were "four to draw to," exceedingly dangerous.

As will also appear, none of them was very bright, and that includes their mother, evil genius or not. Lack of anything resembling a brain is, and was, a common criminal characteristic, and it seems to run in families. But the Barkers were surely persistent in their criminal careers, persistent to the bitter end, as it turned out.

Doc murdered a man in Oklahoma in 1922 and spent the next ten years in "Big Mac"—McAlester Prison, as tough a place as any this side of Alcatraz. Once out, he lost no time in returning to what he did best: brutalizing other people. He ran with several very bad men, including his brother Fred and Alvin "Creepy" Karpis.

Bank robbery was Doc's main occupation, with several murders thrown in along the way, among them a night watchman in Tulsa. Along with Fred, Karpis, and other veteran criminals, Doc hit the big time with the successful kidnappings of William Hamm and Edward Bremer within six months of each other. Both well-publicized crimes produced large paydays, which should have been enough to finance a quiet retirement for the whole family.

For Hamm was the heir to the Hamm Brewery fortune; his ransom ran to a hundred thousand dollars. Bremer's wealthy family was also financed by a brewery, among other things; they came up with twice that much. Now this was 1933–34, when a dollar was really a dollar.

The ransom money was paid in cash. The bills were marked, of course, but there were underworld operators who would swap the hot money for bills without a pedigree, for a substantial percentage, of course. Even so, the ransom should have adequately financed years of outlaw comfort, plus a little frivolity. But Doc and his colleagues didn't learn.

Doc remained a working outlaw until January 1935, when he was collared by the newly christened "G-Men" and hauled off to face the rest of his life in prison. It was the formidable Rock this time— Alcatraz—famously escape-proof: If you got past the guard force and the walls, you still had to face the wicked, chilly tides of San Francisco Bay. Nevertheless, Doc tried it in 1939, and predictably he was killed in the attempt.

Brother "Slim" ran with the so-called Barker-Inman-Terrill gang, robbing banks across the Midwest and murdering at least two police officers in the process. At last run down, cornered by police, and badly shot up, he committed suicide rather than face prison. At least he saved the taxpayers some money.

It seems that Ma tried always to be close to her vicious offspring, and she is said to have resented any attention the boys paid to other women. She was already quick with poor excuses for their foul behavior, too: In her eyes there was always somebody else to blame—society, the police, whomever.

That didn't extend to her own affairs, though, for she dumped husband George and got herself a lover along the way. A femme fatale she wasn't. Any photograph of Ma suggests how unlikely a passionate *liaison* was, but maybe there was something special about Ma her pictures didn't show.

She was with son Fred when the FBI caught up with him hiding out on Lake Weir, near Ocklawaha, Florida, on January 16, 1935. After much shooting, the FBI closed in to find both Fred and Ma filled full of holes and very dead. The story goes that a Thompson submachine gun was found in Ma's hands—or near her—depending on which version you read. More newspaper space was devoted to a sinister radio that was turned on "all day" and the fact that both of the two Barker cars were equipped with a radio, not a common thing back then.

The press had a field day. For example, the Jacksonville (Florida) *Times-Union* predictably described the federal fire as "withering" and lavished no end of purple prose on the great "six-hour" gunfight, like this: "Machineguns were found beside the bodies of both victims. 'Machinegun Kate' and her son had no intention of being taken alive."

"Machinegun Kate?" That would fit with the myth of Ma as the leader of the pack, vicious to the end; but there's also a theory that J. Edgar Hoover, uneasy about killing a mother—even a Barker mother—stage-managed that incriminating scene, inventing a tale that Ma was found with the "Chicago piano" beside her. And Hoover produced some deathless twaddle about Ma being "the most vicious, dangerous and resourceful criminal brain of the last decade."

Asked about Ma's leadership and planning of the gang's criminal forays, veteran robber Harvey Bailey wrote, "That old woman couldn't organize a meal," or something like that. And Alvin Karpis described "Machinegun Kate" thus: ". . . she wasn't a leader of criminals or even a criminal herself . . . an old-fashioned homebody from the Ozarks . . . superstitious, gullible, simple, cantankerous, and well, generally law abiding." And Alvin was in a position to know.

"Machinegun Kate" Ma Barker certainly wasn't. But the whole era has produced reams of "historical" prose on the Barkers, and there has been much speculating about Ma's status and other details of the Lake Weir fight. Certainly Hoover produced a great deal of prose about that battle, all of it plainly calculated to inflate the role and reputation of the FBI and, not incidentally, his own. This in addition to being a neat apologia for the death of somebody's mother.

And as usual the movies have had a field day with the Ma Barker story, also as usual with not a whole lot of attention to accuracy. One of the really enjoyable films was *Bloody Mama*, starring Shelley Winters, complete with submachine gun. It's occasionally on television, and if you don't take it as serious history, *Bloody Mama* is well worth watching.

So ended the road for Ma and three of her poisonous brood. That left Lloyd William, who would be the last of the Barkers. He answered to either "Bill" or "Red" and was a veteran of service in World War I; he actually received an honorable discharge.

He was left out of much of his siblings' nefarious doings, having been laid by the heels after a 1921 mail robbery in Baxter Springs, Kansas. That got him twenty-five years in Leavenworth, where he remained until the autumn of 1938. Red went back to the army and worked as a cook during World War II, gaining not only another honorable discharge but a Good Conduct Medal.

He took a job at a Denver bar and grill when he got out and lived on until the spring of 1949, when his wife became sufficiently irritated with him to blow him away with a shotgun. The lady was not operating on all eight cylinders, it appears, but Red remained dead nevertheless.

So passed the Barker boys and their momma. Other gang members came to similarly unpleasant ends. Alvin Karpis—sometimes called Old Creepy—was in the thick of many of the Barker clan's lethal adventures. A dedicated career criminal, he deserves a few words of his own.

Karpis was Canadian by birth, but he fit right in with all-American hoodlums like the Barkers and the punks who ran with them. His éminence grise was Fred Barker, with whom he shared some jail time and a budding career robbing banks. By the end of 1931, they were wanted for several robberies and the murder of at least two law officers.

For a while they had lived with Ma at White Bear Lake in Minnesota. Nobody knew them there, and they could busy themselves with housebreaking and other minor crimes. Karpis hungered for more. And so, early in 1932, along with Fred, the murderous sadist Larry DeVol, and two other men, he drove south to Concordia, Kansas, to hit a bank.

The planning was elaborate, involving carefully casing the bank, holding a getaway rehearsal, and stashing gasoline cans at appropriate spots along the line of retreat. They even left coffee and sandwiches at one of their gas dumps; you had to feed the inner man, after all. They paid great attention to detail, right down to a supply of corks, to plug any gas-tank holes police bullets might make, and overalls, the better to blend in with the bucolic nature of the town.

The robbery went like clockwork, and the gang quickly cleaned out the tellers' cash drawers. Customers and staff were herded into a back room, and the only bank employee who knew the combination to the vault was ordered to open it. Then came the snag. "No," quoth the bank man simply, and no amount of death threats to himself or his coworkers could change his mind.

He is quoted as simply explaining his position to the outlaws, who blustered loudly and positively clanked with weaponry: "I ain't openin' no vault for anybody." No amount of tough talk could change his position, including Fred's gun-brandishing and the murderous DeVol's threat to burn out the stubborn bank man's eyes.

And so the great criminal planners had to run without their big payday for which they had so carefully plotted. They had gotten more than twenty thousand dollars in loot from the cash drawers, but that seemed pretty small potatoes after all that planning. Curses! Foiled again!

Other small bank robberies followed, but the end of the rainbow remained elusive. And so, in December 1932, the gang tried the Third Northwestern National Bank of Minneapolis. This time it would be Doc and Fred Barker and an assortment of other punks, including one with the curious nickname of "Lapland Willie." As usual, they were armed to the teeth: Their arsenal included no fewer than four submachine guns—anybody could buy one in those less-regulated days, even by mail order.

Karpis was probably along, too, although he later said he wasn't; his excuse was that he had to go and assist Ma Barker, who, he said, told him she had had a heart attack. Nobody wants to admit to being part of murder, even Karpis. For that is what happened.

In the first place, the building lacked cover and

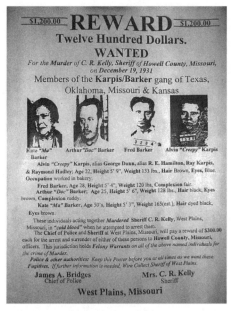

Barker wanted poster

concealment; it was, as Karpis put it, "like working in a greenhouse." Worse, somebody triggered the silent alarm and a pair of officers drove up in front of the bank; they had no chance. DeVol and another punk sprayed their car with tommy gun fire, and both officers went down, one dying, the other mortally wounded. The fat was now well into the fire, and to compound the problem, as the gang switched cars during the getaway, a stranger drove slowly by.

Fred assumed he was writing down their license number. The man wasn't. He was a Good Samaritan who had merely slowed down to see if these people needed help. What he got was not thanks, but a fatal bullet from Fred's pistol. Now every man's hand was against the gang, if it hadn't been before.

After some R&R out in Reno, it was back to the old grind again, a series of holdups more or less successful, and the gang's pièce de résistance, the Hamm and Bremer kidnappings. Throughout this time and afterward, Karpis assiduously reinforced his own myth.

He was, he said, something of a latter-day Robin Hood, taking from the rich and giving to the poor, helping all the poor people forced off their ancestral land by those heartless banks. That was arrant nonsense, of course, but in those hard times it appealed to a lot of ordinary folks.

The bank raids continued, with uneven success. One holdup netted two whole bags of . . . worthless checks. And then there was the matter of Dr. Joe Moran, through whom they tried to launder some of the stolen money. Dr. Moran, an apparently competent physician, was also a lush, who had futilely tried plastic surgery to change the appearance of both Fred and Alvin. He did, however, manage to erase Alvin's fingerprints, scraping off the appropriate patches of skin.

The good doctor might have gone on making a fine living making felons' prints go away. But his boozing and drunken babbling raised questions about his discretion, and he ended up in Lake Erie. He was quite dead, of course, and without his hands and feet, an apparent attempt to hinder identification.

Karpis stayed free for another sixteen months or so after the Lake Weir fight, until the FBI caught up with him in New Orleans in May of 1936. He was taken without a fight, allegedly personally captured by J. Edgar Hoover. The other version of the apprehension tells that other agents safely secured Karpis, and only then did Hoover appear to formally arrest him.

Hoover certainly made much capital of the event, however it really went down. He and the Bureau got the glory, and Karpis got a long stretch in the federal prison system. He went off to join his old buddy Doc Barker, who had already gone to Alcatraz the year before and who would die in his abortive escape attempt in 1939. Karpis would spend the next thirty-some years in the federal prison system, most of it on The Rock.

Finally paroled, Karpis was deported to his native Canada, and he ultimately died in Spain, where he busied himself with books . . . about himself, of course. While in Alcatraz he took pity on a young convict who'd spent a lifetime in various institutions. Karpis decided to "do something for him" and began to teach the youngster to play the guitar. Karpis later said of his young charge, "There was something unmistakably unusual about [him] . . . a runt of sorts, but found his place as an experienced manipulator of others. I did feel manipulated, and under circumstances where it hadn't been necessary."

It is small wonder that even the experienced Karpis felt manipulated. The punk he had befriended was named Charles Manson, as weird and murderous a psychopath as ever walked, who became the mystic guru of a band of murderous misfits. Oddly, the last lair of Manson and his ghoulish entourage would be called . . . Barker ranch.

There were other men who honed their skills with one or the other or all of the Barker gang. Most of them were predictably vile specimens of humanity, but one stands out and deserves special mention. On an ascending evil scale of one to ten, he rates an eleven. He was Larry DeVol, and what sets him apart from his crooked contemporaries is not that he was a killer. Lots of outlaws were killers . . . but DeVol liked it. A lot.

DeVol murdered a police officer in Kirksville, Missouri, and left a trail of dead from there before he finished his earthly race on the dirty end of a policeman's bullet. Before the world was rid of him—at only age thirty-one—he was responsible for the deaths of at least eleven people, six of them lawmen.

As early as 1929 DeVol met the noxious Alvin Karpis—in prison, from which the two escaped. Recaptured in 1930, after his release DeVol was back doing what he did best. In March 1932 he reached the big time of crime when he joined other charter members of what came to be called the Barker-Karpis gang in their first major crime. It was a whopping score for the time, more than a quarter-million dollars

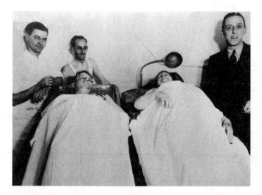

Ma & Fred Barker, extinct

in cash and bonds. In October of the same year, he was in on a Minnesota bank robbery that netted a paltry $4,400. To these high-livers, that was just walkin' around money.

And finally, just four days before Christmas, he was captured in St. Paul and ultimately convicted of both robbery and murder. The sentence was life, but he later showed signs of mental problems—feigned or real—and was moved to an asylum. He escaped and went back to his usual profession of robbery, until the summer of 1936, when he fought the law in Enid, Oklahoma, and this time the law won. Sadly, a police officer died, too, before this thoroughly worthless hoodlum went down.

Thus passed the Barker gang, who left a trail of corpses across the Midwest and attracted a series of equally worthless helpers. Nearly everybody who ran with the Barker gang ended up dead, most of them early in life. Nobody mourned their passing very much, but the grief they left behind for other people was incalculable.

Robin Hood and His Merry Men they weren't.

CHAPTER 11

Bad to the Bone

The Selman Brothers

Much has been written about the most famous outlaws like Billy the Kid, the Daltons, the James boys, and their ilk, as a sort of aristocracy of western bad men. They were that, if aristocracy is the word for the top of the heap of scum, but there were a good many others like them who were every bit as big a boil on the behind of the body politic. They include such men as John Larn and Mysterious Dave Mather, Dirty Dave Rudabaugh and Deacon Jim Miller, and any list of them also has to include the Selman boys, John and Tom Cat. Although John acquired a good deal of renown and a good deal of praise for exterminating the deadly John Wesley Hardin—who surely needed killing—most of his life was a darker chapter.

John Selman was born in Madison County, Arkansas, in 1839, to the respectable family of his English father, who taught school and farmed on a small scale on the side. And then, when John was about nineteen, the family moved to Grayson County, Texas. John had four siblings by this time, one of whom was a brother, christened Thomas. After his father died, John became the man of the house, and he remained so until the Civil War turned everybody's life upside down. John joined a Confederate cavalry outfit stationed in Oklahoma, but by 1863 he'd had enough of the military life and deserted to move the family to a Texas town near Albany.

There he apparently had second thoughts about martial glory and enlisted in a state militia outfit. He seems to have been popular, enough so that after the quaint custom of the day he was elected lieutenant by his peers. By 1865 he had married, and four years later he moved the whole family group off to a spread in Colfax County, New Mexico. Any attempt to found a new life there was frustrated when hostile Indians ran off the family livestock, and so it was back to Texas, settling not far from Fort Griffin, a wild town in the running for the wickedest town in western America . . . which is saying something.

John showed his combative streak early. He is said to have killed several hostile Indians during raids around Fort Griffin, and there is a high probability that he put an end to the earthly life of a local bad man called Haulph, or something similar. He also met some genuine tough guys, men such as Wyatt Earp and Doc Holliday, Deacon Jim Miller and Bat Masterson. By now John surely belonged to the unofficial fraternity of hard hombres. He was in good company.

Another of John's associates left a good deal to be desired in terms of social standing, for he kept company with a local harlot familiarly and intriguingly known around town as Hurricane Minnie. Minnie, obviously, was for fun, but for business he became a close friend of John Larn, a very deadly bad man indeed.

Larn ran cattle, and he had even spent some time as sheriff of Shackelford County . . . after all, he may have considered that line of work a socially acceptable guise for bringing down his competition, particularly in that part of the world. As he and Selman became closer and closer friends, they began, it was rumored, to increase the size of their herds by some midnight requisitioning of other folks' stock. Larn was conveniently a leading member of the Tin Hat Brigade, whose function was the suppression of rustling. A number of suspected rustlers ended up decorating trees in the Fort Griffin vicinity, some with brief explanations of the reason for their demise. One such epitaph is worth repeating: "He said his name was McBride, but he was a liar as well as a thief."

John Selman owned a saloon, ran some cattle, and invested in lots around the town, but his main business seems to have remained rustling, in partnership with Larn. Until, that is, Larn's long career in larceny caught up with him in the form of a posse that blew him away while he was in custody in the local jail. The catalyst for his demise was the discovery—significantly weighted down in a creek on his property—of a number of hides from cattle that did not carry his brand.

Selman was on the vigilante list, too, but warrants for his arrest were never served, he having witnessed the arrest of Larn and learned from it. He departed the Fort Griffin area in some haste, and while he was "on the scout," his wife died, pregnant with their fifth child. So Selman, now in company with his brother Tom—known as "Tom Cat"—drifted into Lincoln County, New Mexico, where John collected a group of hoodlums to prey on honest people. "Selman's Scouts" were a holy terror to honest folk; they robbed little country stores and ran off other people's cattle until the army got into law enforcement and the "Scouts" disintegrated.

By 1879 Selman had organized another gaggle of hoodlums out in West Texas, and they robbed and pillaged until John came down with a prime case of smallpox. Once healed, he raised still another gang of outlaws, who thrived for a time until Selman was arrested in Fort Davis, cutting short the honeymoon for his two-day-old marriage. At that he was lucky, for Tom Cat got himself lynched. Once behind bars,

John Selman WESTERN HISTORY COLLECTIONS, UNIVERSITY OF OKLAHOMA LIBRARY

Selman is said to have bribed his jailers; he escaped and had the good sense to adjourn in haste into Mexico.

Once safely in Chihuahua, he opened a new saloon and went prospecting. He sent for his family, too, including son John Jr., of whom more shortly. Once the heat was off, he returned to the United States and opened still another saloon in Fort Bayard, New Mexico. That is, until he was involved in a shooting and felt moved to return to Mexico, where he sold, of all things, John Deere farm equipment.

By 1888, once he heard there were no more charges waiting for him in Texas, he and two of his sons returned to El Paso, then as wide open a town as the United States could boast of. For a while he worked for a smelting company, and then he moved on to leading a couple of cattle drives. He got himself stabbed in the face along the way, but he survived and became the city constable in 1892.

In 1893 he remarried, choosing as his bride a sixteen-year-old girl—he was fifty-three—and then, in the next year, he killed ex–Texas Ranger Bass Outlaw in a celebrated incident. Outlaw, who liked booze a lot, was a nasty piece of work when he was drinking, and one night during an argument in Tillie Howard's bordello, he fired a shot, apparently in high dudgeon because his favorite harlot was busy. His shot brought Ranger Joe McKidrict, who knew Bass and did no more than ask, "Did you fire that shot?"

Outlaw snarled, "You want some too?" and promptly killed McKidrict with a shot to McKidrict's head and another into his back. Selman intervened, but a round from Outlaw's pistol nearly blinded him with close-range powder burns, and two more slugs badly wounded Selman in the leg. But Selman's return fire tore into Outlaw's chest, and the ex-Ranger died that night, his last couch a harlot's bed . . . well, that's where he wanted to be, wasn't it? His last words were said to be, "Where are my friends?"

Selman continued on as constable, although the leg wounds from Outlaw's gun left him badly crippled; he walked with difficulty, using a cane the rest of his life, which wouldn't be long. He was aging visibly now, and becoming more and more truculent, as if he felt the need to prove how tough he was over and over. But his most memorable hour was still to come, the 1895 encounter with storied gunfighter John Wesley Hardin.

John Selman Jr., recently appointed to the El Paso force, had arrested one Beulah Morose (also M'rose), a soiled dove married to rustler Martin Morose. It seems Beulah had been playing footsie with Hardin, moving Hardin to anger against the Selmans, and one version of the story tells that the falling-out was aggravated when Morose was shot down on the Rio Grande bridge and the killers took from his body a good deal of money. The facts are convoluted and unclear to this day, but it appears that they may have agreed to split the money with Selman and then reneged on the agreement.

Whatever the truth, Old John Selman's hour had come, for on an August evening in 1895, Selman walked into the Acme Saloon, where Hardin was shooting dice with another man. "Four sixes to beat," Hardin crowed to his competitor, but the man didn't have to beat anything, for about that time Selman put a bullet into the back of Hardin's head and then, taking no chances, pumped two more rounds into him as he lay on the saloon floor. About this time John Jr. rushed into the saloon and grabbed his father's arm, stating the obvious as he did so. "Don't shoot him any more; he's dead." And he was. He ended up planted close to Martin Morose.

Under the circumstances of the killing, Selman was charged with murder, the evidence made stronger by the fact that neither of Hardin's two pistols had been fired, or even drawn, although witnesses were found that said they had been. But the jury could not agree on either guilt or innocence, probably because the deadly Hardin was about as welcome as the flu, and the general El Paso public's verdict was something akin to: "So what? Who cares?" Still, to a reasonable observer the first jury had been dead wrong, and so a retrial was scheduled.

It didn't happen, for in the spring of 1896, Young John got his tail in a crack down in Mexico. It seems he had become enamored of a Mexican girl in El Paso, all of fifteen years old, and the two bicycled off to Mexico, intending to find somebody to marry them, or so the story went. They were unsuccessful, and so the two did what came naturally and sought a hotel for the night. But the girl's father found out about their plans, the Juarez mayor showed up with some help, and Young John ended in the *calabozo*.

Old John visited the boy in that dismal jail and said he would return to work things out, bringing Deputy Marshal George Scarborough with him. Old John never returned, however, for very early on Easter Sunday, Selman got crossways with his fellow lawman Scarborough at the Wigwam Saloon. The cause of the quarrel is said to have harked back to the Morose affair and the question of the split of Morose's money after he was killed. Scarborough was supposed to be in for a cut of Morose's money, too. Whatever caused the falling-out, Scarborough put four rounds into Selman, apparently without any sort of warning. In spite of a doctor's attempt to relieve his paralysis by removing the bullet pressing on his spine, Old John Selman didn't make it.

He left a goodly number of very dead bodies in his wake, but it sure had been a colorful ride; there weren't many like him.

CHAPTER 12

England's Rejects

Ben and Billy Thompson

They came from a good family, sons of an officer of the Royal Navy who emigrated to America with his family in 1851. They settled in Austin, Texas, where they had kinfolk, and there sons Ben and Billy grew up.

Ben, the elder, born in 1842, seems to have been reasonably intelligent, but he also had a marked propensity for trouble. He wasn't afraid of working, as so many budding outlaws were; it wasn't that so much as a sort of combative spirit that led him into a series of shooting scrapes. He went to school for several years and later worked as a printer and bookbinder in Austin and New Orleans.

When the Civil War broke out, Ben joined the Confederate army and served in the Southwest. Even in uniform, his pugnacious nature got him into more trouble, including a couple of "shooting scrapes." He was also involved in various distinctly unmilitary activities, such as high-stakes gambling and a bit of whiskey smuggling. There was another shooting incident just after the war; this one got Ben jailed, but he managed to bribe a guard and took "leg-bail" along with several others. Texas seeming somewhat inhospitable, Ben went off to Mexico.

That much-troubled little country was then in a state of civil war, and Ben chose the wrong side, enlisting in the army of the French-supported-usurper "Emperor" Maximilian. Ben was even commissioned, but that proved an empty honor when the French gave up their dreams of empire and abandoned Maximilian, whom the Mexican opposition not only caught, but shot.

So back went Ben across the border and back to gambling, apparently his first love. He returned often enough to his second, fighting, finally doing two years for threatening a justice of the peace. It all started when Ben's brother-in-law hit Ben's wife, and Ben went after him.

Ben pulled his trusty pistol and fired several shots at his brother-in-law, but only, as Ben said, to just "scare him," which no doubt it did. One round inflicted a slight wound, and Ben turned himself in to the JP. An argument ensued, during which Ben, never a model of restraint and discretion, threatened to kill the JP. His companion-in-mischief was his younger brother Billy, whom Ben had managed to rescue from a murder charge.

When Ben saw daylight again, he headed for friendlier climes, in this case Abilene, Kansas. That was Ben's kind of place, a booming rail-head town, destination of the big trail herds up from Texas, swarming with rowdy young cowboys.

Ben opened the Bull's Head Saloon with partner Phil Coe—later to be killed by Wild Bill Hickok—and brought his wife and daughter to Kansas. Tragically, the day they arrived in Kansas City they and Ben were badly injured in a buggy accident, with his wife eventually losing an arm. After much hospitalization and treatment, they returned to Texas. But the lure of the money and excitement of virgin

Kansas pulled Ben back, and in the summer of 1873 he was in Ellsworth, another booming railhead town. Billy, the proverbial bad penny, showed up soon afterward.

Now if Ben had some ability at getting things done, Billy was something of a burden at the best of times. He had a profound love for the demon rum, and he was a source of unmitigated trouble when he was full of strong spirits, which was usually. Ben had already bailed him out of trouble at least once, and it was about to happen again. In spades.

Billy's victim this time was E. B. Whitney, the much-respected sheriff of Ellsworth. It happened when Ben had gotten crossways with local badge-wearing hoodlum Happy Jack Morco and a man called Sterling. The unarmed sheriff tried to cool things off, but Morco and Sterling attacked Ben and Billy, and in the resulting confusion Billy put one barrel of a shotgun into the lawman.

There are several versions of the tale, but at least one thing is consistent. When Billy's shotgun downed the sheriff, Ben Thompson, horrified, exclaimed, "You've shot our only friend!" Billy, drunk as usual, was belligerent and unapologetic, also as usual. "I'd have shot Jesus Christ!" he said, or words to that effect.

The killing of Sheriff Whitney did not sit at all well with the citizenry of Ellsworth, and Billy left town at the high lope; so did Ben, by way of Kansas City and other towns. Ben managed to salvage Billy from a homicide charge in the Whitney killing in Ellsworth, and he went back to gambling and, increasingly, boozing.

Ben's luck finally ran out in San Antonio in March of 1884. He was out on the town with John "King" Fisher, a Texas gunfighter as deadly and well-known as Ben was. Both men had downed a few, and they decided to wrap up their evening at the Vaudeville Theater and Gambling Saloon, a substantial place of entertainment that featured such headliners as Eddie Foy. It might have been a pleasant time; trouble was, the year before Ben—then city marshal of San Antonio—had

Ben Thompson WESTERN HISTORY COLLECTIONS, UNIVERSITY OF OKLAHOMA LIBRARY

exterminated one Jack Harris, a proprietor of the place, and Harris's friends and successors had not forgotten.

Why Ben took the chance of going to the Vaudeville at all defies explanation; maybe it was pure arrogance, maybe it was simple contempt for Harris's survivors. Those men were, however, not only hungry for revenge but most unwilling to give Ben an even break. The *National Police Gazette* put it well: "His desperate ferocity when roused, his fearless disregard of his own and other lives, and his fatal proficiency in the use of the revolvers were too well known to fail in acting as a warning to the employees. . . . From the moment of his entrance to the theatre he was a doomed man."

And so he was, and King Fisher with him, for the two fearsome gunfighters were ambushed somewhere on the theater's dress circle in a blast of point-blank firing, at which, said the *Gazette,* the other theatergoers hastily took flight: "The dress circle was quickly cleared, the occupants jumping into the parquet below and through the side windows into the street."

It's not certain whether either of these veteran gunmen even got off a shot; Fisher, at least, never got his gun out of its holster. Both were quickly down and dying; Fisher had been hit thirteen times, while Ben took nine rounds.

A Vaudeville employee named Joe Foster took a bullet in one leg, and, as the paper dispassionately put it, "will probably die of hemorrhage." Sure enough, Foster died of the wound and subsequent amputation.

One version of the fight is that Foster quarreled with Ben, who pulled a revolver and jammed it in Foster's mouth. Another Vaudeville man "grabbed the cylinder of the revolver," and a struggle ensued. Several other men joined in, including a performer at the theater and storied gambler Canada Bill.

Brother Billy, as usual a day late and a dollar short, showed up after the shooting stopped and accomplished nothing save getting himself arrested. Billy's career—if you can call it that—ended in obscurity. Without his big brother to rescue him from trouble, he was headed for more, and eventually he found it.

But along the way he is known to have soldiered in the Civil War as a member of the Texas Mounted Rifles, where he served in Louisiana and soldiered with brother Ben along the border. The two are said to have found time to run a monte game, at least until Billy killed a soldier and Ben helped him escape up to Indian Territory, long a ready-made refuge for the lawless.

Billy followed Ben around in the years that came after, first as a dealer in the Bull's Head and later in Ellsworth, where he murdered Sheriff Whitney. On the run, he next turned up in Buena Vista, Colorado, where, one story tells, he became mayor. This in spite of a five-hundred-dollar reward offered by Kansas, where he was wanted for Whitney's death. Some three years later he was caught in Texas and returned to Kansas, only to be acquitted.

He showed up in Austin after that, and later followed big brother to Dodge City. After a time he drifted to Nebraska, where he is said to have been wounded five times in an Ogallala gunfight. That town being distinctly unfriendly—folks were talking about lynching—Billy "took it on the heel and toe," as the saying went. He had the competent assistance of Bat Masterson. Bat, who wasn't known in Ogallala, came from Dodge City to help out at Ben's request; another saving of the family wastrel by long-suffering big brother.

Billy came full circle after that, returning to San Antonio in time for his brother's murder at the Vaudeville. Not being armed, for a wonder, he could not take immediate revenge, and his arrest gave him some time to think about his own future. With no Dutch courage inside him, he never went after the men who killed his brother.

In 1882, however, he was in Corpus Christi long enough to be accused of yet another killing, and he wisely traveled on to El Paso, where he remained for several months. Nobody is sure where and how Billy ended his wasted life. It was probably in Laredo in 1888 or thereabouts.

It's uncertain how many shooting scrapes Ben was involved in over the years. He is known to have killed four men for sure, and probably two more, in a career that included more than a dozen gunfights. Since people back in the nineteenth century generally didn't keep minute records of such deadly doings, the death toll could well have been far higher, and, knowing Ben, probably was.

The brothers' careers on the wrong side of the law lasted longer than those of most of their violent contemporaries, and left more corpses in their wake. Maybe somebody mourned their passing . . . but probably not.

CHAPTER 13

A Vanished Yesterday

The Sutton-Taylor Feud

Most people have heard of the Hatfields and McCoys, the "feudin' mountain boys" of song. Some know about the Lincoln County War out in New Mexico, mostly because it involved Billy the Kid. But not so many outside the great state of Texas have heard of the Sutton-Taylor feud, which over the years involved hundreds of men, good and bad, and left a substantial trail of dead over three decades.

The feud kicked off in 1865, in the bitter days after the Civil War. It had its center in DeWitt County, about halfway between San Antonio and the Gulf of Mexico. There were small farmers here and there, but most of the land was given over to stock raising. After the Civil War, all across the western United States change was on the way. So was big trouble.

The Suttons and the Taylors were substantial cattlemen who didn't like the disintegration of their seignorial society. The black population

was no longer as subservient as once it was; Union troops were enforc-
ing the law, searching people for weapons; and to make matters worse,
there was a series of bad crop years.

Some folks emigrated, but some old families like the Taylors and
Suttons stayed, being naturally stubborn folks, and maybe longing for
a vanished yesterday. They began to prosper again in 1867, when the
cattle boom really began, the days of the huge herds moving north
along the great trails to feed the insatiable eastern hunger for beef.

Five Taylors had settled around the town of Cuero: the brothers Pitkin, William, Josiah, Rufus, and Creed, all surrounded by
ever-extending families. Two of Creed's sons, Hays and Doboy, were
blacklisted by the Union occupiers and intelligently headed for the
high lonesome, as the saying went. They were joined by a number
of other young men who had the misfortune to make the same list.
Their exile put something of a cramp on their ordinary activities; for
instance, Doboy had to wed his light o' love at night, with both bride
and groom on horseback.

Things really came to a head in the fall of 1867, when some Union
soldiers began to push Hays around in the little town of Mason. Hays
killed one soldier, and a friend got another. A Union major tried to
arrest Hays and was promptly shot down. Other murders followed,
including the ambush of a Captain Littleton and another man on the
San Antonio road. Littleton had been heard to say, about arresting the
Taylors, "I will do it or die." It turned out to be "die." Nobody saw a
Taylor at the ambush site, but . . .

The Taylor clan was targeted in the spring of 1869, being considered part of the general unrest and outlawry that plagued post-
war Texas. The military governor cannot be blamed for acting, but his
choice of agents was unfortunate.

They were a couple of professional shooters, the most notorious
of whom was "Captain" Jack Helm, who had the reputation of being
as willing to kill you as look at you. Helm, the ace man hunter, was an

abominable sort on his best days. He is said to have murdered a black man simply because his victim whistled a "Yankee song."

He and his colleague—C. S. Bell—were the sort of men the word "pompous" was designed for, but deadly as well. They raised a posse—at government direction—which may have been as many as fifty men strong. This force, rejoicing in the inevitable nickname of "regulators," went on a rampage that led to the deaths of at least twenty-one people and the apprehension of another ten. Some of the dead were clearly rustlers and similar ne'er-do-wells, but some of them weren't.

Some of those killed—the general public view was that the deaths were murder—were adherents of the Taylor clan, and that meant that the Taylors, if they hadn't been wholeheartedly in the scrap before, certainly were now. They came in for sure after the next chapter, which was nothing less than a well-planned raid on the very heart of the Taylor clan itself.

The Taylor menfolk already slept out in a pasture away from the family home, so they could not be surprised in their beds. However, the regulators moved in on the Taylor place at night, when only the Taylor women were at home. And when their menfolk came home next morning, the regulators were waiting. As they approached the house, Doboy's wife ignored the guards watching the women and screamed loudly. Doboy, already dismounting, heard her warning, jumped back in the saddle, and vamoosed with only a superficial graze to one arm. Hays, however, charged a line of shooters behind a fence, according to the Galveston *Weekly Civilian*, "wounding five of them and being himself literally shot to pieces."

Doboy, after being wounded yet again elsewhere, lasted until the autumn of 1871, when he picked a fight with the wrong man in an unrelated matter. Doboy pulled his pistol, but his tough assailant won the encounter.

As with many other things connected to the feud, there are two versions. One is that Doboy's revolver misfired and his enemy's didn't.

The other is that his foe jumped a fence, wrenched Doboy's revolver from his hand, and killed him with it. However it happened, Doboy remained dead.

By that time the feud had taken on a life of its own, with family loyalty, ego, and bitter memories making it almost impossible for either side to quit. Bill Sutton had inserted himself into the mix by joining a large posse that chased a band of rustlers and caught up with a couple of suspects in a town called Bastrop. One was killed when he "tried to escape," and he turned out to be named Charley Taylor. The Taylor family said he wasn't one of theirs—although other men said he was.

The Taylors said the feud had begun in earnest when Buck Taylor was shot down on Christmas Eve of 1868 by Bill Sutton's men. Or maybe not. There are even stories that the feud began back in Georgia long before, or maybe it was someplace in the Carolinas.

The battle certainly heated up in 1870 when the Texas State Police were created. The sort of lash-up that organization was can be judged by its leaders, one of which was the murderous Jack Helm, who set about recruiting the same sort of hoodlums who had formed his last posse—that included Jim Cox, already detested by the Taylors, and Old Joe Tumlinson, a noted Indian fighter who generally packed three or four guns. Direct Sutton involvement came about with the addition of Bill Sutton.

In August, two Taylor in-laws named Kelly were "arrested" in Sweet Home, Texas, for disturbing the peace and were murdered on the road, at least one of them by Bill Sutton. The Taylors and much of the rest of the public were incensed by the grand jury's failure to indict, and things went from bad to worse. The public outcry got so loud that Helm was fired . . . which made little immediate difference, he being also sheriff of DeWitt County. What his departure did do, however, was to elevate Bill Sutton to prominence; if it hadn't been the Sutton-Taylor feud before, it sure was now.

Pitkin Taylor departed this life after a night ambush in 1872. Lured out of his house by the sound of a cowbell, he incautiously took his shotgun and went outside to see what was the matter. Several gunmen promptly shot him down before he could get his finger to the trigger. He lingered for half a year, but his death added even more fuel to the family fire.

One tale tells that during Pitkin's funeral, a group of Sutton partisans drank and hooted and rejoiced nearby. Nothing they could have done was better calculated to infuriate Taylor souls, and Bill and Jim Taylor swore to take vengeance. "I'll wash my hands in old Bill Sutton's blood," said Jim to his mother, and he meant it. At least one good thing came to pass: Over the governor's veto, the Texas legislature managed to abolish the state police.

In the spring of 1873, Bill Sutton survived a Taylor attack in a Cuero watering hole called Banks' Saloon and Billiard Parlor; badly wounded, he recovered enough to murder a couple of Taylor men the following June. Another try at killing Bill failed. About this time deadly John Wesley Hardin became a Taylor partisan, if he hadn't been one before. There was a sort of distant family relationship here, too: Hardin's cousin had married a Taylor daughter.

In July 1873, Jim Taylor and Hardin found Sutton thug and Regulator leader Jack Helm in Albuquerque, Texas. Although Helm had six men with him, Hardin's trusty shotgun blew Helm away, abetted by several bullets from Jim's revolver, equipment that substantially outweighed Helm's knife. The six "allies" departed without waiting to try conclusions with Hardin and Taylor.

A sort of truce followed, which the Gonzales *Inquirer* opined "would be rigidly observed." In his splendid book *I'll Die Before I'll Run*, C. L. Sonnichsen cogently observed, "One of the laws of feuding seems to be that a truce holds only long enough for the signers to take cover."

This one lasted all of three months. It was back in high gear by December, when a pitched battle raged around the Gulf Hotel in

Cuero, after a running fight that started around the courthouse down the road in Clinton. The Clinton citizenry, including the local judge, asked the combatants to take their feud someplace else. And the slaughter continued elsewhere: In January 1874, four men were killed in a single week. Cuero was relatively peaceful, thanks in part to the citizens of the Cuero Protection Club, who warned all and sundry to take their damned war elsewhere.

Later in the year, Hardin killed a Brown County deputy sheriff and produced a prodigious backlash from the local citizens. Ultimately four more men were lynched and all of DeWitt County became an armed camp, until the state sent in a group of about forty Rangers under the formidable Captain McNelly. Their presence and professionalism were the beginning of the end for the bloodshed that had gone on so long.

But the Taylors weren't through. The following spring, Hardin alerted Jim to the chance to at last murder Bill Sutton, which they promptly took. At the same time they shot down Gabe Slaughter, apparently an innocent friend. This killing was particularly ugly in Texan eyes because the murder was committed on a steamboat in the presence of Sutton's wife and child, or pregnant wife, depending on the version of the tale.

The murders of Sutton and Slaughter would not be forgotten by the Suttons, so retribution was, as usual, not far behind. In June the Suttons lynched three Taylor partisans, including a Taylor with the unfortunate name of Scrape, or Scrap. The impromptu hanging was answered by the murder of Rube Brown, the Cuero town marshal, who had earlier arrested Jim Taylor.

The whole dirty mess ended with a sort of *Götterdämmerung* two days after Christmas 1875, in Clinton, Texas, when a Taylor party led by Jim left their horses with the wrong man, either a false friend or a coward, or both. When a Sutton group appeared, shooting of course, the horse-minder promptly abandoned his charges, and the horses intelligently departed.

Left afoot, the Taylors were surrounded by the Sutton men, and the inevitable end followed: the extinction of Jim and his men. With the departure of Jim, then the leader of his clan's warriors, the feud petered out, although isolated acts of violence continued. In later years, both families produced a multitude of outstanding citizens for the Lone Star State, including Jim Taylor's brother Bill, onetime feudist who ultimately died in action as a lawman.

Nobody knows for sure what the final death toll was, although the estimates run as high as forty dead, without considering the widows, the orphans, the home burnings, and the stock killings.

Attila would have felt right at home in DeWitt County.

CHAPTER 14

Just Plain Nasty

The Casey Boys

The Casey clan lived near El Reno, Oklahoma, on a stream called Mustang Creek. They started their criminal careers early, when they were suspected of killing two neighbors, bachelor brothers, apparently to get the brothers' farms. Old man Casey and one of the sons had been tried for the murders and acquitted, after which the family prudently moved farther to the west.

There is a story that some years earlier, near the family's previous home down in the Arbuckle Mountains, the family patriarch had murdered two old men, assisted by his toxic sons Vic, Jim, and Dave. Another tale tells that even earlier the family had murdered "several pedlars" in the same area. One may wonder about the veracity of that, because at the time Vic would have been about eleven years old, and Jim only three years or so older. But maybe the kids were just along for the ride, or the old man took them with him to learn the niceties of murder and robbery.

The Casey boys enter this story during the night robbery of a Rock Island train at Pond Creek in April of 1894. The leaders of this raid were a well-known hoodlum called Felix Young and one Nate Sylva, an ex-con suspected of fencing stolen stock for the Dalton brothers.

They recruited several other men, apparently including the Casey brothers, and a couple of them boarded the train when it stopped at little Pond Creek for water. Down the track a short way, the two threw down on the train crew and forced them to stop, at which point the rest of the gang came running out of the darkness yelling and shooting.

Inside the express car were express messenger John Crosswight, and the guard, Jake Harmon. At first they did not yield to demands to open the express car, until at last the bandits planted dynamite at the car door and touched it off. The door remained closed, although the express packages were scattered around the car and Crosswight was stunned. "Open up!" yelled voices outside. "Or we'll throw explosives right on you."

"All right," said Crosswight, "hold on, I'll open the door."

Meanwhile, Harmon had slipped out, making his way through the cars behind the express car and emerging into the night with his trusty shotgun. He spotted three outlaws shouting orders and nailed one of them—a man called Rhodes—with a load of buckshot. The bandit went down and stayed down, and his companions panicked, got quickly on their horses, and clattered off into the night.

About this time a Pond Creek posse showed up, alerted by the train conductor, who had run back down the track to flag down an approaching freight train. The posse ran down one outlaw as he fled madly down a road. He told them he was just a hobo hitching a ride, but he was clanking with weaponry, gave several names, and convinced nobody. So who were the other bandits?

A pair of suspicious-looking characters appeared in the little town of El Reno on May 21, and they seemed to be giving particular attention to the jail. The local sheriff was suspicious and so, when the two left town, a deputy trailed them. They had told the deputy they hailed from the even smaller settlement of Chickasha and were bound for Enid, but when they left town they headed the wrong way, along the railroad line toward Yukon.

The deputy saw the two "make signals to someone on the coaches," and when the train reached El Reno, it was found to be carrying none other than the harridan wife of Nate Sylva, whose husband had also been swept into the bag by the law. It looked as if an escape attempt was in the making. The local sheriff wired Yukon to alert Deputy Sheriff Sam Farris there, and Farris found the pair and told them they were under arrest. He signed his own death warrant.

One of the pair wheeled on Farris and shot him in the groin. The tough deputy was able to draw and return the fire, and one of his bullets hit an outlaw in the foot. As Farris fell dying, the wounded outlaw hobbled away while his companion, spraying bullets, ran for their horses. The wounded hoodlum did not get far, for Farris's brother ran into the street and tackled him, holding on until other citizens could get there to help.

At this, the second outlaw opened fire on Farris's brother and the others, and one round ricocheted from a nearby mowing machine and fatally wounded a bystander, an old man named Snyder. But then a citizen opened fire on the second outlaw, and when he saw other citizens beginning to gather weapons, he quickly got on his horse and galloped out of town. A big posse was right behind him, but lost him in darkness in the thickets along the South Canadian River.

Yukon citizens were understandably angry, and so the wounded outlaw was moved to the guardhouse at Fort Reno as a precaution against an impromptu necktie party. He would not give his name, but Deputy Marshal Chris Madsen saw him and knew him immediately as Vic Casey. It followed that the escapee was his brother, James Casey, and the hunt was on.

Madsen gathered a posse and picked up the fugitive's trail in the brakes of the South Canadian. The pursuit covered just over a hundred miles, ending predictably at the Caseys' new place west of the town of Arapaho. The posse swept up James Casey and turned for home.

Both Caseys denied any wrongdoing, but it wouldn't do either one of them any good. Vic's foot wound got worse and worse and blood poisoning set in, until at last it killed him. His brother's lawyer moved for a change of venue to Oklahoma County, and James was moved there in 1894. He ended up sharing a cell with brothers Bob and Bill Christian, whose names belied their dispositions, and who appear elsewhere in this book.

The Christian brothers had also been transferred to the Oklahoma County Jail in Oklahoma City, which in those days was a two-story building fitted with interior steel cages and considered a secure lockup.

Since neither Casey nor the Christian boys were happy in jail, Bob prevailed upon Jessie Finlay, his girlfriend, to smuggle in several guns, which he stashed in the stovepipe inside his cell. The outlaws chose Sunday, June 30, 1895, to make their break, for on Sunday jailer J. H. Garver allowed his prisoners to move about in the corridor outside their cells. Garver was an easygoing sort, or maybe just plain negligent, because only the day before the Pottawatomie law had wired him, warning about the planned jailbreak. He paid no attention.

He should have. Once Casey and the Christian boys pistol-whipped the jailer and ran into an alley behind the jail, they looked for transportation. Bill Christian found a horse and vanished. Brother Bob and Casey stuck up a couple in a buggy, but the driver wouldn't give up the reins in spite of two bullet wounds. Chief Jones ran toward the buggy and Casey shot him down. He sank down against a building and was dead within five minutes.

A small war followed along Grand Avenue, pitting the fugitives against police officers Stafford and Jackson and several armed citizens.

The lawmen drilled Casey through the neck and head, and the desperado died in the riddled buggy.

The Casey boys weren't around long, which was a good thing for everybody. But themselves.

CHAPTER 15

The Plague of Cochise County

The Clanton Clan

No time or place has gotten so much print or so much film as the Earp days in Tombstone. Most of it has cast the Earps in the role of the Good Guys, often without much if any regard to their human shortcomings.

Two superb recent films, *Tombstone* and *Wyatt Earp*, have stuck by the Good Guy image, although without glorifying the brothers overmuch, and at the same time giving a fair picture of Doc Holliday, especially Val Kilmer's portrayal. Kilmer's Holliday will ever be remembered with his classic line, delivered after Wyatt's "single-handed" defeat of the Iron Springs ambush. Asked where Wyatt is, he replies, "down by the creek, walkin' on water."

The Earp brothers seldom appear in popular print—still less in the movies—as "The Fighting Pimps," only one of the less-than-flattering names their foes and detractors gave them. And indeed, the fact is, they were men of their time, far from perfect.

Wyatt Earp, as he
appeared 1886

Wyatt Earp WESTERN HISTORY COLLECTIONS, UNIVERSITY OF OKLAHOMA LIBRARY

So if the Earp party constituted the Good Guys—and that seems to be a fair portrayal by and large—who were the bad hombres? If Wyatt and his brothers were on the side of the angels, who were the villains of the piece?

The answer, in print as in film, is ever the Clanton clan: N. H. "Old Man" Clanton and his noxious brood. In their day, however, not everybody in Arizona subscribed to that notion. If you were part of the so-called "Cowboy faction," your view was different.

The Clantons came to southern Arizona in 1877, where the patriarch of the family, Old Man Clanton, bought a ranch. He seems to have operated it with son Billy's help, while sons Isaac (always "Ike") and Phineas ("Phin," of course) went into the freighting business. They also operated a part-time and more profitable family enterprise, regular raiding into Mexico, where there were lots of valuable cattle to be rustled.

These they peddled north of the border, and they were joined in the rustling by as unsavory a group of misfits as could possibly have collected in one place: John Ringo, Bill Brocius, Frank Leslie, Frank and Tom McLowery (sometimes McLaury), and a number of others of similarly larcenous persuasion, none of them anybody you'd want to invite home for dinner.

For a while, the wild town of Tombstone was their oyster, a wide-open place of twenty-four-hour merriment and considerable killing. Boot Hill was filling fast—it's a tourist attraction these days—and the local law—in the person of Sheriff John Behan—was tolerant if not actually complicit. Since struggling small ranchers in the area grew their herds in part on the illicit traffic in beef, they tended to side with the rustlers.

Understandably, northern Mexico's rancheros were not pleased with this wholesale rustling, nor with the murder that sometimes accompanied it. In July of 1881, for example, the Clantons waylaid a group of Mexican cowboys driving a herd through Guadalupe Canyon and are said to have murdered nineteen of them.

Tombstone, major streets 1879–80

Just a few weeks later, a band of vaqueros—or maybe it was *sol-dados*—ambushed the Clanton clan and their cowboys on the way home with a stolen herd. They blew away five of them, including Old Man Clanton himself. The shooting occurred on the American side of the border, also in Guadalupe Canyon, long the scene of considerable bloodletting.

Leadership of the clan now descended to Ike Clanton, one of the truly poisonous characters in the history of the western United States. His portrayal in *Tombstone*—as a bully, a criminal, and a coward—seems to be right on the money.

Once the Earp brothers appeared in Tombstone, the high-handed behavior of the Clantons and their mangy friends hit a snag. Their buddy, Sheriff John Behan, who did little or nothing to enforce the law as to the cowboys, was obviously only a talking head. The Earp boys, however, ably supported by Doc Holliday, tended to do unfriendly things like pistol-whipping noisy and recalcitrant cowboys, especially if their names were Clanton. The Earps had the support of Mayor John Clum and much of the town's population.

After some sore heads and time in jail and similar frustrations for the Clantons and their friends, it inevitably came to open war, but exactly how that sparked is forever lost in the mists of time and the mythology that tends to grow up around any notable event in the Old West.

For what followed was the famous, deadly confrontation at Tombstone's OK Corral—not *in* it as so much popular "history" has it. There are—of course—two wildly different versions of the encounter. In one, the Clantons and their friends are mostly unarmed; they don't want to fight; they protest that they are peaceful, but in the end they are shot down mercilessly by the brutal Earp party.

In the other version, the Cowboy party spends the day bragging in the hearing of other citizens about how they'll exterminate the Earps and Holliday. They send word to the Earps that they're down near the corral and ready to fight, and so on. If that's the case, then the fight that follows is entirely the Clantons' fault. Virgil Earp summons them to surrender, holding out his gun hand in a gesture of peace and persuasion.

At the hearing before Judge Spicer, other witnesses testified to the Clanton bunch making threats to Virgil and his brothers. There were a number of witnesses who testified they saw the gunfight, or parts of it, but there was no agreement about who shot whom and when they shot them. Ike Clanton, of course, blamed everything on the Earp party and said the whole idea of the Earps was to kill him.

A woman with a clear view of the fight may have given the most compelling testimony, among other things that: "The cowboys opened fire on them, and you never saw such shooting. One of the cowboys after he had been shot three times, raised himself on his elbow and shot one of the officers and fell back dead."

In the end, Judge Spicer exonerated the Earp party; Virgil was, after all, an officer of the law. He had every right to stop the Clanton bunch and arrest them for possessing weapons in the city, which was a clear violation of the law. Spicer's opinion is worthy of a partial quote: "Isaac Clanton could have been killed first and easiest. If the object was to kill him, he would have been the first to fall. . . . I cannot resist firm conviction that the Earps acted wisely, discretely and providentially to secure their own self-preservation."

Judge Spicer seems to have examined the evidence with great care, concluding among other things that the wounds to Frank McLaury and Billy Clanton could not have been received if they were in the midst of trying to surrender, as Ike loudly asserted.

The county grand jury, which could have overridden the judge's tentative findings, chose not to. Doc and Wyatt were safe from the law, but not out of danger. The feud wasn't over, of course. There were death threats to several citizens, including Judge Spicer.

Even the town newspapers took sides: The *Epitaph* supported the Earps and the decision by Spicer and the grand jury. The rival *Nugget* as usual took the opposing view. The small ranchers tended to support the "Cowboy faction," while the town's citizens welcomed the extinction of the Clanton bunch, that perpetual irritant to the public peace.

A large funeral procession and public finale for the three dead cowboys hadn't helped cool things off at all. The remains had first been laid out for public view gussied up in new suits, under a big sign proclaiming that they had been "MURDERED IN THE STREET OF TOMBSTONE."

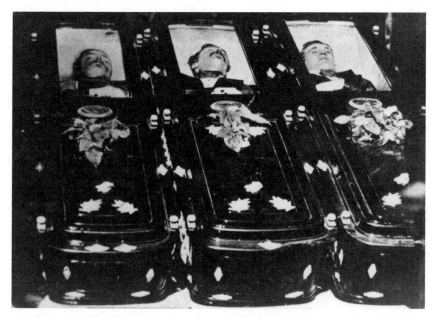

The losers from the Earp-Cowboy fight WESTERN HISTORY COLLECTIONS, UNIVERSITY OF OKLAHOMA LIBRARY

Nobody will ever know precisely what happened in this the most famous of all western gunfights. The Earp version of the tale is far more persuasive, and it has considerable support from the citizen witnesses. And it's doubly convincing for another simple reason, which the mass of writing usually tends to overlook: Only one of the Earp party had anything but a revolver.

Had a group of experienced gunfighters gone to the OK Corral *intending* to kill a group of probably armed enemies, surely everybody in the Earp group would have carried a shotgun, far and away the best close-range weapon ever devised. Not only is the shooter virtually certain of a hit, he can count on doing enough damage that his opponent doesn't have the strength to shoot back.

Although the legends—both ways—will never die, the shootout is a matter of fairly straightforward history. Ike Clanton survived the fight, pleading loudly that he wasn't armed, moving Wyatt Earp to famously declare, "The fighting has now commenced; go to fighting or get away!" Or something like that. Whereupon Ike the blowhard fled the scene, taking refuge at Camillus Fly's nearby photography emporium.

Ike did indeed "get away," but his brother Billy did not. One version of the battle has Billy shouting "I don't want to fight!" and being blown away all the same by Morgan Earp. Billy had more than his share of guts: Even while wounded once and shot again, he was on his back trying to shoot at the Earps when Tombstone photographer Fly courageously ran between the warring parties and grabbed Billy's gun from his hand.

The aftermath is fairly straightforward, continuing with the murder of Warren Earp and the crippling wounding of Virgil from ambush. The rest of the story, the "vengeance ride" of Wyatt and his friends, is better documented, with a good deal less myth and invention than the fight and its causes.

The old Cowboy faction was gone now, even John Ringo, mysteriously dead with a bullet hole in his temple and a pistol in his hand, sitting in a faraway canyon, his boots mysteriously missing, his feet wrapped in rags. He was murdered, some say, maybe by Wyatt or Doc, maybe by Johnny-behind-the-Deuce or Buckskin Frank Leslie. Or maybe somebody else. Or he shot himself. Nobody will ever know. Or care.

Phin and Ike Clanton left the Tombstone area, moving some two hundred miles north to Apache County. There they went to ranching, but old habits die hard, and they couldn't seem to keep their hands off other people's stock. And so, in the summer of 1887, they were faced by a stock detective and his posse. Phin wisely surrendered, and he would get ten years' hard time. But the poisonous Ike either went for his gun or tried to flee or both. It was a bad idea, whatever it was, and the world was finally rid of him.

Whatever the true sequence of events was before and during the fabled gunfight, it seems certain at least that it would not have happened without Ike.

Not much of an epitaph.

CHAPTER 16

Two-Bit Tough Guys

The Martins

There wasn't much to like about the Martin boys. They didn't have any use for the law, and none at all for other people. Most of the trouble they got into early in life was penny-ante, hitting the bottle, tearing up small towns, and pushing ordinary people around. But they graduated to the big time in the spring of 1899.

When they left petty crime for what they thought were broader worlds, Will was about twenty years old, an arrogant hoodlum with a nervous tic on the left side of his face. Brother Sam was older, a tobacco-chawing dolt no brighter than his brother. The opportunity for their elevation to really serious crime was the law-abiding Hull family, honest folk and good citizens, everything the Martin brothers were not.

One day while the Martins were hoorahing the town of Mulhall, in Oklahoma Territory, all the gunfire and yelling stampeded Hull's livestock. Hull filed formal charges against the two hoodlums, but the law failed to act. The brothers Martin were angry that anybody even challenged them and were determined to punish Hull. And so they stopped Hull and his family on a country road, and their anger at the farmer showed plainly. For after he had filed charges against them, they had already attempted to take their anger out on Hull's hide once, but the big farmer proved too tough for them. That must have been a crushing blow to the brothers' egos. They did not forget.

On the lonely road, Hull was helpless. The brothers were armed to the teeth and Hull was not. And he had his family with him, his little daughter and his pregnant wife. And so Hull offered the brothers what little money he had, but they wanted more. "Get out of the area in five days or come up with $150," one of the brothers ordered. When the farmer protested that he would have to sell his farm to raise that much, Sam told him that if he didn't do as ordered, they would dynamite his farm.

Hull didn't have that kind of money—very few people did—but he tried to borrow it. He didn't have the credit, however, and he followed the banker's advice and went to see the law. He was afraid to sign a complaint, but the local deputy sent three lawmen off to investigate. Hull went along to show them the way to the Martin farm out on Skeleton Creek. The brothers weren't there, a resident said, but they had moved on to another farm, owned by the Simmons family. The law followed.

When the three deputies arrived at the Simmons place and called on the brothers to come out, the two ran out the back door and the officers gave chase. The Martins opened up on them, and the officers shot back. One lawman's shots knocked Will down, hit by ten or twelve buckshot, and Sam was seen to stagger as he ran to safety.

Will was caught and charged, but for some incomprehensible reason the grand jury failed to indict. Recovering from his wounds, Will left Mulhall and rejoined his brother. The two hoodlums were just getting started.

The Martins traveled up through No Man's Land—the long western panhandle of the Territory—and ultimately into little Cimarron, Kansas, west of Dodge City. Along the way they equipped themselves with a pair of 1895 Winchester rifles, and Sam got himself a memorably beautiful Colt revolver with stag-horn grips. They held up several little stores and isolated farm families as they worked their way up the Arkansas River, and as they went along, people noticed the beautiful Colt and the two new rifles. If the brothers were trying to cover their tracks, they were doing a lousy job of it.

They made it back to Oklahoma Territory in March 1903 and invaded the train depot at Hennessey. Somebody recognized them and audibly murmured "the Martins," but the outlaws could not identify who had spoken. One of the four men present in the station noted that the smaller of the robbers had a facial tic. That tic fit Will, and it would confirm the identity of the bandits.

The depot robbery didn't pay off in booty. The cash drawer had a measly $8.35, and the bandits went to work on the safe, hacking away with a hammer and crowbar and getting nowhere. They also tore apart some packages in the freight office. And then they killed a man, a harmless civilian who did not threaten them.

The victim was a young black man named Gus Cravatt, who was minding his own business until somebody across the street in the darkness yelled at him to halt. He thought one of the railroad men was joking, and as he was crossing the railroad track, a rifle bullet tore into his thigh. A night watchman responded to Cravatt's cries, and he was shot at, too. He returned the fire until his pistol jammed. The outlaws ran then, got to their horses, and galloped off into the gloom.

The watchman and some citizens carried the young man to his father's house, and two doctors did their best for him. They could not stop the gush of blood from a torn artery, however, and Cravatt died. When daylight came the next morning, a large, angry posse took up the chase, as the fleeing outlaws repeatedly abandoned exhausted horses and stole new ones. At one point the law got close enough to exchange gunfire with the outlaws, but the pursuers could not bring their quarry to bay.

Near the town of Marshall, the posse again got into a firefight with the fugitives, but the exchange took place at about three hundred yards and nobody was hurt—at that range, with the firearms of the day, a hit would be either lucky or accidental. The posse lost the trail again after that, but the law would not quit.

The local Anti-Horse Thief Association set about warning ranchers and farmers in the area, but the outlaws stole still another team from a farmer and showed their small-souled dispositions by also rustling a batch of spareribs the farmer's wife had cooked for her husband. The pursuers found the farmer's buggy broken down and abandoned and tracked the outlaws farther, following discarded sparerib bones.

The robbery had occurred on a Monday night. On Saturday the chase was still on, and still another inconclusive gunfight with lawmen took place near the tiny town of Isabella. Again nobody was hurt and the robbers broke contact, stole more horses the next morning, and ran again, all the way down into the Texas Panhandle.

Exactly where the brothers went is unknown, but history does show that they rendezvoused with Richard Simmons, a dirtbag who had deserted his family down in Logan County, Oklahoma. Simmons fit right in.

Now the brothers demonstrated their acute mental vacuity. Instead of leaving Oklahoma far behind them, the outlaws moved their base of operations into the rugged Osage, in northeast Oklahoma Territory. The Osage country was a thinly settled, tangled, difficult land that had been and would remain an outlaw haven. It was a country of rock and thick groves of trees, brush, and ravines, a very bad place from which to root out armed fugitives. For the moment, the brothers were safe from the law, but then they threw that opportunity away.

The gang made quite a splash with their next undertaking, a wholesale criminal enterprise seldom seen before. They found a spot along the road between the towns of Bartlesville and Pawhuska and robbed one traveler after another, Simmons guarding each one of their victims in a thicket of trees while the Martins watched the road for more travelers. Among the victims was a onetime deputy marshal named Dave Ware, traveling with his wife. Sam Martin recognized Ware and crowed, "You're a killer; why don't you do something?" Ware wasn't having any. "To hell with you," he said. "You've got the drop and I have no gun." And he added ominously, "I'll wait."

But the bandits had more plans for wholesale robbery. One of their victims was driving a hay wagon, which the Martins soon turned into a barricade across the road. By six in the evening, the bandits had collected an astonishing bevy of captives, some one hundred men, women, and children. They had also acquired more than fifty horses, not to mention all manner of buggies and wagons. It had been quite an afternoon and the outlaws disappeared again, moving far to the west.

Their next target was the tiny town of Hopeton, a hamlet south of Alva, and there they invaded a combination store and post office, stealing about a hundred dollars, a batch of postage stamps, and some clothing. They took a couple of shots at a man driving by in his wagon when he would not stop. They missed him, and he clattered off down the street. The robbers fled, and this time they had about a ten-hour start on a pursuing posse. Again they disappeared, only to surface near the thriving railroad hub of Geary.

Geary already had two banks, and somebody was building another one. The town even rose to the dignity of having a good-size hotel and its very own opera house. It also had its share of saloons and plenty of violence. Such a tough town required tough law enforcement, and Geary had exactly that.

The city marshal, John Cross, was quite a character, hardy and courageous, the epitome of the Western-movie lawman. When Cross became a little dry, he would ride his horse into a saloon, collect a beer, and ride on out the back door. Even with little peccadilloes like this one, he was a popular man.

The Martins and their hanger-on Simmons had their eyes on the town's twin banks, but their appearance aroused some suspicion. A young farmer spotted them on his way into town but did not surely recognize them for what they were. He did, however, remember that one man carried a beautiful Colt with stag-horn grips. Neither the farmer nor another man who saw the gang was entirely satisfied with their appearance, and they intended to tell Marshal Cross about the strangers the next day.

But that night the lawman did not return to his farm outside of town. When he was about four hours overdue, his worried wife saw his horse come home, wounded and without its rider. She telephoned the town, and people turned out and began to look for Cross. They found him all right, but he was dead, shot through the body, and they also found what remained of a fire and signs that three men had been there. The inescapable conclusion was that the marshal, doing his job, had ridden up to the fire and simply been shot down.

A large posse gave chase, led by Sheriff Ozmun of neighboring Canadian County. The trail led south toward the town of Anadarko. While the posse was on the trail, rewards totaling $1,350 were offered by the territorial government, the county, the local Independent Order of Odd Fellows (IOOF) lodge, and the Anti-Horse Thief Association.

For two weeks lawmen pursued the gang, running down reports of sightings. It was learned that the outlaws had intended to stop and rob a Santa Fe train but called off their attempt when they learned that the train carried guards. They contented themselves with robbing a cowboy at the 101 Ranch and pushing on.

And then the officers got a break, a report that the outlaws had returned to the rugged Osage country. There are several versions of how this came about. The news was passed along either by an Indian who had fed the three, by cowboys who recognized them, by a doctor, or by women sent by the foreman of a cow camp at which the gang had bullied the camp cook into providing them meals.

Once in the Osage, the posse discovered the outlaws with help from a group of Osage Indians. These Indians had watched a heavily armed white man come down to a creek to draw water. One of the Osages followed him some eight miles and then rode into Pawhuska to find deputy Indian Agency police chief Wiley Haines, who also carried a commission as a deputy US marshal. The Indian reported what he had seen to Haines and even drew a little map of the location of the outlaws.

Haines collected Osage chief of police Warren Bennett and Indian policeman Henry Majors. The three officers rode casually out of Pawhuska and headed for a piece of high ground deep in the ravine of Bird Creek. The little knob of ground, thick with brush, was called Wooster Mound, and the lawmen timed their arrival to reach the area at dusk. In the failing light they dismounted behind the last ridge between them and Wooster Mound.

Crawling forward to the ridgeline, they found their quarry, settled down and relaxed, one man watching the horses while the other two hunkered down behind a pile of saddles and other gear and cooked something over a small fire. Much later, a Lawton deputy named Woody added a few details to the story. The officers saw the smoke from the outlaws' fire, he said, and crawled closer to find their quarry dining on grilled meat.

But then one of the bandits' horses saw or smelled Haines. The beast snorted, and the fight was on. Sam Martin grabbed his rifle and sprang to his feet, already firing, while his brother grabbed his own weapon and made a run for the creek. Haines and Bennett stood up and charged into the open, firing as they went.

Haines hit Will in the leg and then hit him again in the corner of his mouth, a bullet that also removed a substantial portion of the back of his head. He fell into a ditch, quite dead. Meanwhile, Bennett was shooting at Sam, hitting him in the wrist and in the right shoulder, a round that continued on to exit from his chest. Sam went down as well, falling in a patch of shade.

Haines pulled his revolver and cautiously approached the motion-less outlaw. But then, as Haines got close, Sam Martin rolled over and fired. Haines started to jump away when he saw Martin begin to move, which may have saved the lawman's life. As it was, the wound he received was ugly. The soft-nosed slug tore into his shoulder and swerved toward the back of his neck, leaving a deadly trail of frag-ments from the bullet's copper jacket. Some scattered into the officer's right lung, tearing at the blood vessels.

As Haines fell, Bennett rushed past him, kicking the outlaw's rifle away and promising Martin a bullet between the eyes if he tried any-thing more. Meanwhile, Simmons was running for his life. Officer Majors pulled down on the man with his rifle, and the bandit fell. But he immediately jumped up and continued running. In reporting the battle the *Oklahoma State Capital* noted that the combatants had fired a total of twenty-seven rounds in a single wild minute and lauded the "[t]hree brave and nervy officers who took on three desperadoes who had sworn never to be taken alive."

The Osage Indians, still in their nearby camp, appeared and loaded Sam Martin and the badly wounded Haines into a wagon. Bennett performed some crude emergency surgery on his deputy, cutting at least some of the rifle bullet out of his shoulder. Haines was still in desperate straits, however, and needed immediate medical attention.

Bennett and Majors collected the booty: three horses (all stolen), a heap of tack (also stolen), weapons, camping gear, and some thousand rounds of ammunition. Prominent among the captured weapons was Sam's fancy Colt revolver with its stag-horn grips. The lawmen also found Sheriff Cross's star and silver watch, both stolen from the fallen lawman.

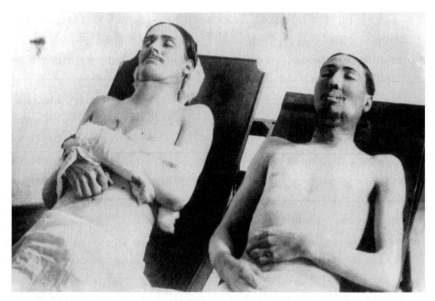

The Martin boys WESTERN HISTORY COLLECTIONS, UNIVERSITY OF OKLAHOMA LIBRARY

Haines teetered on the edge of eternity but slowly improved.

Not so Sam Martin. As he slowly sank, Sam told the law all about the gang's depredations. He told of the Hennessey robbery and the murder of Gus Cravatt, the wild afternoon of multiple robberies on the Bartlesville road—"more than a hundred people," he boasted— and the robbery of the post office and store at Hopeton. He could not resist boasting that he, his brother, and Simmons had robbed "more people than any gang in history."

And finally, looking death in the face, he added, "I guess I've been on the wrong trail."

He sure had.

There was, as the *Oklahoma State Capital* put it, "great rejoicing" among the populace at the extirpation of the Martin boys, and the remains of the outlaws were hauled into Guthrie so that their identity could be confirmed. A number of their victims identified the corpses as the men who had robbed them, the brothers were carted off to the ministrations of Patterson Brothers multifaceted entrepreneurs with their undertakers' hat on, and the *State Capital* again waxed eloquent in praise of the lawmen, especially their wounded leader: "An honest man is the noblest work of God."

It fit Haines precisely.

CHAPTER 17

The Kansas Horror

The Bloody Benders

In the years just after the Civil War, the so-called Western Movement accelerated as great waves of people headed west, as the saying went, "to seek their fortune." Many of them were new immigrants, looking for a better life in this new land of promise. A man could settle on a piece of land and make it his own, no landlord, no crop sharing, no kaiser, no czar, no duke or whoever, nobody to tell a man what to do.

To the waves of pilgrims from the settled East of the United States and the hungry newcomers from across the wide ocean were added many people from the defeated South, leaving a ruined, defeated land for a new start. One hundred sixty acres of their very own just for the "proving-up" was a glowing dream to most of the families moving west.

Most of these people were solid citizens, the salt the western earth was hungry for, willing to work any number of hours in all kinds of weather to build something for themselves, something to have and to hold, something of value to leave to their children. Most of them were devout people, people who wanted to live in peace and follow the law, divine and terrestrial. They were the ideal material to build a great nation.

But there were the others. Along with the good, God-fearing people came the criminal scum, not interested in hard work, or for that matter in work of any kind. Many were fugitives from prosecution or from jail in distant parts. What all of them came west for, besides refuge from the law, was a consuming interest in what they could take away from people who worked for it, and sometimes in simply gratifying their own egos by brutalizing others.

But the Bender family was different. They were "spiritualists" for one thing, and over time the four family members exuded an aura of intense evil not common even in the tough, wild land west of the Mississippi. Their crimes were plain enough, murder and larceny; it was the rest of it that turned other people's stomachs.

The Bender family's lives otherwise remain a profound mystery. In the first place, it is unclear whether they were in fact a family at all. The patriarch was a hulking, unsociable brute of a man—somebody described him as "like a gorilla." He spoke a gutteral, virtually indecipherable variety of what in those days was called Low German.

Referred to as "beetle-browed John" and otherwise known as Pa Bender, he was perhaps sixty years old. His dumpy wife, inevitably "Ma," was somewhat younger, maybe fifty-five, so unsociable and withdrawn that some folks called her the "she-devil." Ma Bender declared herself to be psychic; she spoke to the spirits, she said, and maybe she thought she did, given what happened later on. One neighbor put it neatly: "We thought Mr. Bender was an ugly cuss, but she's no improvement."

There were two children—or at least they were believed and held out to be children—son John and daughter Kate. John was given to

Kate Bender

Kate Bender KANSAS HISTORY

oft-repeated spasms of giggling, which led some people to think, as one author quaintly put it, he was "a few bricks shy of a full load," but Kate was much admired, being called beautiful and voluptuous among other good things. She was also, it appears, something of a flirt, but she had her darker side—much darker, as will appear.

Like her sullen mother the lovely Kate also boasted of her prowess in talking to spirits, even devising a handbill calling herself, rather grandly, *Prof. Miss Katie Bender*, and advertising her ability to "heal all sort of diseases; can cure Blindness, Fits, Deafness . . . also Deaf and Dumbness . . ." She is said to have journeyed to small settlements round about to demonstrate her clairvoyant powers, "curing" the sick and holding séances with a variety of spirits.

In short, the whole family was a spooky lot, including the much-admired Kate. But then, people lived much farther apart in those pioneer days, and it took longer to get to know even your neighbors at all well. Today, when all the evidence is in that ever will be, there is some evidence that the Benders were not a family at all.

Pa Bender may have been born Flickinger. Ma, it is said, was named Almira Meik; she had been married earlier to one Griffith and produced twelve children, one of whom was Kate. There is also a tale that Ma had been married a number of times before Pa, and that each of her prior spouses "died of head wounds." Giggling John, says another story, may have been Kate's lover or husband.

The men filed on adjoining homesteads in what would later become Labette County, Kansas. The area was very sparsely peopled when the two male Benders arrived in the autumn of 1870; it had been much fought over by frontier guerrillas. In the words of one early resident, the area had been "made perfectly desolate" by the year the Civil War ended. But now eager pilgrims were coming in ever-mounting numbers.

Pa and John settled two adjoining parcels of 160 acres each, one of which was a long, narrow strip running beside the Osage Trail, which led from Independence, Missouri, northeast to St. Paul. It was regularly used by travelers of all kinds, and that was probably its attraction. The Bender men built a sixteen-by-twenty-one-foot single-room house by the road, complete with a tiny basement about seven feet wide.

The basement could be entered by either a trapdoor in the house floor or either of two exterior doors, which seem always to have been locked. There was also a sort of tunnel, which may have been used to lever in a monstrous seven-foot slab of rock, which became the cellar floor . . . or maybe it had other uses, too.

The house was to serve as the family dwelling. It would also do further duty as a sort of primitive country-store-cum-bed-and-breakfast, advertised by a crude sign that read "Grocry" until Kate turned the sign over and neatly spelled "Groceries" correctly. The Bender womenfolk arrived some time in the winter of 1871, and their crude hostel was soon open for business. Kate spent some time waiting tables at the restaurant in a hotel in newly minted Cherryvale. That there were then two hotels in that nearby town by December of 1873 is some indication of the increasing traffic on the Osage track. She apparently held the job only a few weeks, until the spirit moved—literally—to start her career as a spiritualist and healer.

So far, although the senior Benders won no popularity contests, at least Pa was known to spend some time reading his German Bible— You can't be *all* bad if you read the Good Book—and Kate and Young John attended Sunday school. But a little at a time the initial good, or at least neutral, impression began to change.

Kate was accused of larceny of a sidesaddle left with her by a woman who used it to secure Kate's healing fee. And a man—probably well in his cups—told a tale of seeing Kate and another woman dancing naked by firelight to strange music. In another report, when a doctor interrupted a Bender healing session with his patient, he was disturbed by the anger he saw in Kate's face.

Kate's spiritualist ad KANSAS HISTORY

Right up there with the naked dancing in the theater of the bizarre was another woman's description of her last visit to the Bender homestead, of witnessing there the Bender men plunging knives into pictures of men drawn on the house walls. That memorably unpleasant evening ended when Kate confided that the spirits told her to kill her visitor, who fled into the night. Consistent with that tale is the story of someone who saw satanic images and figurines in the Bender shack.

Then began the time of the disappearances. During the terrible winter of 1872, two men turned up with their throats cut and their skulls fractured. Later that year a man named John Boyle disappeared after he set out to buy some land, and he was carrying almost $1,900 to finance his real estate transactions.

On and on those and other unsettling stories continued to circulate in the Cherryvale area of Labette County, rumors of travelers disappearing without a trace. As early as the autumn of 1869, one Joe Sowers had set out for Kansas and simply vanished. So did a man called Jones somewhat later. He later turned up, what was left of him, in a water hole, with a smashed skull and his throat cut all the way across.

And then there was the fop in the chinchilla coat who stopped in at the Benders' place for a drink, the man who drove up in a fine new wagon pulled by two matched horses, and Billy Crotty, who was carrying more than two thousand dollars with him; all vanished. The worst tragedy was George Lonchar, who had lost his wife and was taking his little daughter to stay temporarily with her grandparents; both gone.

Even men of the cloth were not immune, such as Father Paul Ponzilione, scared away from Benders' "Inn" after he saw Pa Bender with a hammer whispering conspiratorially with Kate. And then there was William Pickering, a well-dressed traveler who wanted toast instead of corn bread; he also elected to sit on the side of the table away from the canvas curtain used to separate the dining area from the living quarters, and which he saw had several greasy spots at about head level.

An argument with Kate followed, and at last Pickering announced that if he couldn't eat on the clean side of the table, he wouldn't eat there at all. At which Kate pulled a knife on him, and Pickering departed in some haste. What finally revealed the Bender's reign of terror was the disappearance of Dr. William York, from whom Lonchar had bought a team and wagon before he disappeared with his daughter. When Dr. York heard about the disappearance of Lonchar and his little girl, he rode down to aid in the search. When a half-starved team was found abandoned, he identified the famished horses as those he had sold to Lonchar.

And then the doctor was suddenly gone, too, vanished like the others. There was some indication that he had stopped for the night at the Benders', and he was known to have been carrying several hundred dollars and riding a fine horse. In light of what the neighbors later learned, his possessions and his interest in the Lonchar family were a certain death warrant.

Dr. York's disappearance brought in Nemesis at last. Dr. York's brother, a very tough soldier, Colonel Alexander York rode out to find out what happened to his brother. He brought along still another brother, Ed York, and the persistence of the two spelled the end for the Benders' comfortable life of murder and robbery. The brothers dug so deeply that the Benders disappeared virtually overnight, telling nobody, and leaving starving stock behind them.

For the York brothers had talked to as many residents as they could find, and they had even hired local help to drag waterways and beat their way through thick brush. With a crew that one writer estimated at fifty helpers, the brothers covered a lot of ground, and they didn't look like they'd be stopping anytime soon.

They had interviewed the Benders and had gone away profoundly underwhelmed. The giggling son had invented a fable about himself, a tale about being ambushed and shot at; he even led the brothers to the alleged site of the shooting. The second act had been Kate's boasting about her prowess as a healer and seer. Neither sibling impressed the investigators in the slightest, and it was a given that the older Benders would have created a very bad impression.

No doubt the vexing investigation by the York brothers provided part of the impetus, but what probably told the Benders that the game was up was a mass meeting of local men that resolved that all the residents ought to open their farms to a search. It was apparently unanimously approved, and so the handwriting was on the wall.

The news of the Benders' sudden flight brought neighbors out in force. Once it was certain that the Benders had vanished from their shack, a thorough search was launched. It was not long before a sharp set of eyes spotted a depression in the earth in one of the few small areas ever cultivated by the Benders. The searchers began to probe, and very shortly they uncovered the body of the colonel's brother, buried facedown in a shallow grave.

Nobody could forget the mysterious series of disappearances that had plagued this end of Labette County; now that one body had turned up and there were solid suspects, digging on a larger scale began immediately. Very soon large groups of citizens were turning over the earth near the Bender shanty, shoveling grimly in a stench of putrefaction as they uncovered victim after victim.

How the murders had been committed came slowly to light. When the crude Bender hostel was fitted out for company, a canvas curtain or tarpaulin was hung from the ceiling to separate the minuscule "restaurant" area from the family's tiny private space. The kitchen table sat in front of the canvas, and guests were ordinarily seated at the table with their backs to the canvas. Dinner was served by one of the Bender women, but food was not all some unfortunate guest got.

The story goes that while the guest was being entertained inside, some family member checked his wagon or horse, including his luggage or saddlebags. That gave the family some notion of the desirability of turning him into a corpse; there were always risks, they knew. Sooner or later somebody might come looking for the traveler.

Once the victim was seated at his meal, and his possessions inspected, that set the stage for the hulking Pa Bender. Once the guest was occupied and off his guard, Pa simply stepped up with one of his three hammers and caved in the diner's skull. Maybe he sometimes struck *through* the canvas—there were suspicious stains on it at about the right height; or he simply stepped around it and struck his victim, or both. The grisly details remain unknown.

Then the remains were quickly shoved through the trapdoor into the basement, where one or more family members cut the man's throat. The cellar floor was soaked with blood; the stench was overpowering, and if that were not enough, the searchers found scattered bullet holes, as if hammers and knives had not been enough to finish off some of the tougher victims.

The digging turned up one horror after another. The bodies were largely naked, and at least one had been badly cut up, as if in a fury of anger. If the sight of the corpses and the smell of putrefaction were not enough, what really turned the stomachs of the searchers was the little girl. Alone of all the victims, the little Lonchar girl had not been cut or battered, rather she had been, as the examining doctor grimly concluded, buried alive under her father.

The temper of the crowd was also not improved by the sight of much of the Bender stock, which had simply been abandoned. The family had done nothing to even marginally protect the beasts, not even turn them loose to fend for themselves. The searchers were sickened by the sight of dead animals, and by some still living that had long been deprived of food and even water.

To this day, nobody is sure of the tally of the dead. There is pretty general agreement about the bodies actually found, eleven of them, plus an assortment of body parts which could not be reassembled into a single whole. What happened to the missing pieces remains a mystery. There are any number of stories that more men were killed; one old tale established the tally of victims at "pretty near forty." That same story has Kate sleeping with John, and "whenever she had a baby they would just knock it in the head."

And there may be some truth in the mass of mythology that has followed the killings. One story laments a young married couple who stopped at the Benders and never left, the groom murdered and the bride raped by both John and Pa before she, too, was killed.

It seems reasonable to suppose there were more victims than were ever found. The body parts account for some of them, and considering that murdering strangers was a way of life for the bloody Benders, there is a measurable chance that today's sophisticated electronic gear might reveal anomalies in the old Bender property that could lead to more graves.

Once it was obvious that the Benders had fled, several posses went looking for them. The governor of Kansas announced a reward of five hundred dollars a head, and another thousand dollars came from Colonel York, although the enormity of the family's crimes probably made the money secondary to a burning urge for vengeance. There were arrests and rumors of arrests of other people, none of which came to anything.

Journalists flocked to the scene, and visitors by the hundreds went away carrying a piece of the old homestead as a treasured souvenir. As the Thayer *Headlight* reported, "The whole of the house, excepting the heavy framing timbers . . . and even the few trees, have been carried away by the relic hunters."

The searches for the Benders went on. One story declares that the Benders were run down "on the prairie," killed on the spot, Kate being singled out to be burned alive, the ancient punishment for a witch. Others said the searches found nothing, or that all four Benders were caught and hanged forthwith, without benefit of clergy.

One tale with the ring of truth relates that the Benders got away by train, their progress traced by recollections of railroad employees of their luggage, which included not only a white bundle but a "dog hide trunk," whatever that may be. One search led across the Oklahoma border to the town of Vinita, where pursuing detectives got word of four Germans, the youngest of whom had told a local man that the four wanted to go far west to an "outlaw colony."

The detectives seem to know of this place, a spot where fugitives lived like troglodytes in dugouts—and a place where lawmen who went in stood a very good chance of never coming out again. The search went on, and they found traces of their quarry somewhere north of El Paso. There the searchers gave it up.

There are other variations on the tale, leading to the family's ultimate unhappiness with living in or near the "outlaw colony." This story had Kate leaving first, bugging out with a transient painter, who later

Bender victims' graves KANSAS HISTORY

deserted her. The same tale has the old folks leaving, too, until Pa deserted Ma, taking with him the remaining loot.

Other tales abound. Ma murdered three of her children, goes one such story, because they saw her murder her husband of the day. Pa was a suicide in 1884, or maybe Ma killed him in an argument over their bloody loot. Another story reports that John really was shy some bricks.

There is much, much more to the suppositions about the ultimate fate of the repulsive Benders, all of it entertaining, but far too convoluted to be included here. It has been ably explored by more than one writer, particularly Fern Morrow Wood, in *The Benders: Keepers of the Devil's Inn.*

Whatever the family's subsequent history, one would suspect that it involved a strong odor of brimstone.

CHAPTER 18

The Bumbling Lawyers

Jennings & Jennings, Esq.

Clumsy Elmer McCurdy had to get killed by the law, get embalmed, and become a professional dummy to have any success in crime, but more on that later. Like Elmer, attorney Al Jennings was a considerable embarrassment to the outlaw profession. And like Elmer, he embarked on a second career with his brother Frank, also a lawyer.

Al had been infinitely more successful as a lawyer than he was as a bandit, at which he was a colossal flop. The difference was that, unlike Elmer, he didn't have to get himself killed to change careers. Al managed to reinvent himself, producing not only reams of dubious prose but a movie glorifying his undistinguished past as a criminal.

What really set Al apart was his signal and uniform lack of success at the outlawing business. Christened Alphonso J. Jennings, he was born in 1863 back in Virginia, son of a lawyer. By 1892 his family had moved west and settled in Canadian County, Oklahoma Territory, at

Al Jennings WESTERN HISTORY COLLECTIONS, UNIVERSITY OF OKLAHOMA LIBRARY

the town of El Reno. His father became a judge in the local court, and Al practiced law in the area with his brothers, John and Ed. In time, the family moved north to the town of Woodward.

Now in those days Territory lawyers tended to be a tough and aggressive bunch, and the Jennings boys fit right in. In due course, however, they tangled with one of the toughest of them all, Temple Houston. Houston was the son of Sam Houston, the father of Texas, and he had been both a district attorney and a state senator down in Brazoria County, in a wild panhandle judicial district. Houston was the very picture of the successful frontier lawyer, with his Prince Albert coat, ornate vest, and, of course, Colt revolver. He had also moved north to Woodward, and it was there that he locked horns with the Jennings boys.

The conflict apparently arose over some harsh words exchanged during a hard-fought case involving Houston on one side and Ed and John Jennings representing the other. Houston called brother Ed "grossly ignorant of the law"—which may have been true—whereat Ed called Houston a liar.

Both men reached for their guns, but cooler heads prevented any bloodletting there and then. Now that sort of thing was not uncommon in those rough-and-ready days, but what made the insult particularly bad this time was that after court adjourned, Houston and a sometime client—named, of all things, Love—met Ed and brother John in the Cabinet Saloon.

Predictably one thing led to another, more hard words were exchanged, and everybody started shooting. Ed ended up dead on the saloon floor, and John ran for his life, wounded in his arm and body.

Al wrote later—he wrote a lot in later life—that Ed was "ambushed." However, several territorial newspapers published accounts of the fight that described it as no more than a common brawl, in which the Jennings brothers came in a distant second. One account reported that, at the saloon, "the quarrel was renewed. Very few words passed before all drew their pistols, including [Houston's friend] Love. . . . All engaged

Temple Houston WESTERN HISTORY COLLECTIONS, UNIVERSITY OF OKLAHOMA LIBRARY

in a running and dodging fight except Houston. The huge man stood up straight and emptied his revolver without twitching a muscle. . . . Neither Love nor Houston were wounded although several bullets passed through their clothes and hats."

Al wrote that he was summoned to the saloon, where he knelt piously beside his brother's corpse and "swore to kill the man who had murdered him." Maybe he swore, but he sure didn't try very hard to go seeking vengeance.

Instead, Love and Houston were tried and acquitted, after eyewitnesses said Ed Jennings went for his gun first and may have actually been shot by his own brother. In any case, Al continued to fulminate about killing Houston but continued to do nothing to carry out his dark threats. Instead, he wired another brother, Frank, in Denver, and the two went "on the scout," as the saying went, allegedly to set up a lair from which to sally forth and kill Houston and Love. Houston and his friend weren't hard to find, but somehow the Jennings boys couldn't manage to be where their quarry were at the same time. Instead, the Jennings brothers launched a brief and somewhat ludicrous outlaw career.

They collected some helpers, rank amateurs Morris and Pat O'Malley, and somewhere along the way were joined by perennial Territory bad-man Little Dick West, alumnus of the Doolin gang. They may also have been assisted by Dan Clifton, another real outlaw, better known as "Dynamite Dick," a onetime Dalton and Doolin follower.

Early in June 1897, the new gang held up a store in Violet Springs, one of the Pottawatomie County "saloon towns." They went on to stick up another country store, robbed a "party of freighters" on the road, and then capped their spree by robbing another saloon and all the patrons. With a sackful of money and some stolen whiskey, they headed for the woods to relax and savor their success.

Robbers identified as Al and Dynamite Dick held up a post office at a wide spot in the road not far from the town of Claremore. That brought federal officers looking for them. In his dubious autobiography, *Beating Back*, Al said this raid was only to test out something called a "set-screw," a contraption he said was designed to pop loose locks from safes. This robbery netted seven hundred dollars, which Al, ever boastful, said was stolen "just to pay expenses."

It was a good beginning, since everybody in the bunch was a tyro bandit except for Little Dick and Dynamite Dick. It was also the last major run of success the gang would have, and now the law was looking for them. Chief among the searchers were Deputy US Marshals

Paden Tolbert and Bud Ledbetter, experienced, smart, and tough, and very bad men to have on your back trail.

Ever hopeful, Al stopped a Santa Fe train near Edmond, a town just north of Oklahoma City. Three members of the gang had boarded the train at Ponca City, well to the north, and transferred to the tender when the train stopped for water at Edmond. The outlaws forced the train to halt a little way down the road, where four more outlaws materialized out of the darkness.

There followed much shooting and yelling to cow the crew and passengers and prevent interference with the onslaught on the express car. Bullets through the wall of the car forced the agents to open the door, and the gang entered to claim their bonanza.

So far, so good. But then things went sour when the safe refused to open. The "set-screw" was apparently left behind or maybe it proved to be unsatisfactory; so the gang tried dynamite. Not once but twice they blasted the formidable Wells Fargo safe, but it refused to open. Or maybe, according to another version of their debacle, there wasn't a safe on that train at all. Defeated, the outlaws disappeared.

They were empty-handed from their first try at a train robbery, and they were unsuccessful at simply trying to flag another down—the engineer just waved at them. And so the gang decided that practice might just make perfect; they would try on a train again a couple of weeks later.

This time they chose Bond Switch, not far from Muskogee. The gang laboriously stacked railroad ties on the tracks as a roadblock and hunkered down in ambush to wait for their prey. The train arrived as scheduled, but the engineer, instead of using the brakes and stopping, used the throttle instead. He smashed through the barricade of ties, and the train disappeared into the night.

Unrobbed.

With the law again on their trail, the gang decided to replenish their money supply by robbing the Santa Fe train depot at Purcell, south of the town of Norman. This time they didn't even get started, for a night watchman saw them skulking about in the gloom before they even began to rob anything. The watchman promptly alerted the station agent, who called the city marshal, who showed up with a posse.

Foiled again.

Shortly afterward, one story goes, the law learned that the gang intended to rob the bank in Minco, but the outlaws again were thwarted because a band of citizens mounted a twenty-four-hour guard on the bank. The Jennings boys and company were getting hungry.

By this time, considerable mythology surrounded the gang's operations. Al Jennings wrote long afterward that at this point he and Frank were comparatively rich from train robberies and a bank job down in Texas. Well, maybe. Rich or not, Jennings wrote that they took a six-month trip to Honduras. There they met one William Sydney Porter, better known later as O. Henry, who would go on to write dozens of the world's most memorable short stories. Just now, however, Porter was also on the run, facing an embezzlement rap in Texas.

Early in 1897, Porter came back to turn himself in and face the music, but Jennings, according to him anyway, returned to Texas by way of San Francisco and Mexico City. Whether Al was luxuriating in Honduras, or simply hiding out in penury, he was back with the old gang by October of 1897 and preparing to try another train holdup.

The gang chose a southbound Rock Island train they thought was carrying some ninety thousand dollars, headed for banks in Fort Worth. Al decided to stop this train in broad daylight, on the dubious thesis that the usual guards were only on duty at night. And so, on the morning of October 1 the gang—six men this time—forced a railroad section crew to stop the train. The gang hid themselves behind bandannas, except for Al, that is, who made himself a weird sort of mask out of a bearskin saddle pocket, cutting a couple of eyeholes for some minimal visibility.

Again, a good beginning, although Al's mask slipped sometime during the holdup. And this time Al and his men had brought lots of dynamite. They were resolved not to be stopped again by a strong safe. And so they laid their charge, lit the fuse, and waited for the money. Frustrated, the bandits laid another and even heavier charge, and the whole train shook. But not the safe.

So the gang was reduced to tearing open the registered mail and robbing the train crew and the passengers—more than a hundred of them—of their cash and watches. Along the way one of the outlaws shot off a piece of ear from a passenger who was slow to cooperate, but he was the only casualty.

This unusual daylight robbery brought lawmen in swarms, several posses converging by train on the outlaws' probable escape route. In addition, the American Express Company and the Rock Island ponied up a reward, eight hundred dollars a head for every outlaw, a good deal of money back then.

But at least the gang got away, ending up circling back to a farm near El Reno, home of a farmer well-disposed to them. There they rested and split up the loot. Moving on, in the cold weather of late October, they moved east toward the town of Cushing, and there they sought sanctuary from the chill and an infusion of money at the home of one Lee Nutter, a local merchant.

They did this simply by waking Nutter, shoving a pistol in his face, and demanding that he go to his store at the front of the building and give them his money. But there wasn't any, for Nutter had sent his store's receipts on to the bank in Guthrie. So the gang had to make do with a couple of weapons and a whole fifteen dollars, plus stealing a jug of whiskey and a selection of coats and such from the store's stocks. The pièce de résistance of their loot was a bunch of bananas. It was another failure, but it was as close to a success as this inept gang would ever have again.

Dynamite Dick and Little Dick West left the gang at about this time somewhere around Tulsa, disgusted with all that work and danger and hardship for no reward. They split up, and Dynamite Dick headed in the direction of Checotah. Early one morning he rode past two deputy marshals—Hess Bussey and George Lawson, lying in ambush waiting for him to appear.

The marshals offered Dick a chance to surrender, but he was wanted for more than the gang's amateurish crimes. There was a warrant for him for a murder committed back in his days with the Doolin gang. With nothing to lose, the outlaw whipped up his Winchester and fired. A return shot broke his arm and knocked him from the saddle, but he regained his feet and staggered into the brush, leaving his rifle behind.

The marshals followed, trailing him by spatters of blood, but the trail was hard to stick to. And then, as night fell and it seemed they had lost him completely, they came on a cabin in the woods. Nobody answered their summons to surrender, until they fired warning shots and announced that they intended to burn the cabin to the ground.

At this a woman and a boy came out. The officers twice commanded them to set fire to the cabin, and on the second command Dynamite Dick ran from the door, shooting as he came. The officers quickly put several holes in him, and he was dead within minutes.

Thus passed Dynamite Dick, veteran of dozens of outlaw forays including the fight at Ingalls in Oklahoma Territory, in which three deputy marshals died, as well as of the bank holdup and murder at Southwest City, Missouri.

Little Dick West was next. Heartily sick of the inept Jennings and his crew, West agreed to help the law entrap the gang, which was again planning to rob a gold shipment. The gang had assembled at the ranch owned by one Red Hereford, but they left at the high lope just before the marshals' posse arrived.

Which only delayed the reckoning a little. On November 29 the gang was holed up in a ranch house owned by a Mrs. Harless. After they had eaten the evening meal, they were visited by a neighbor. He had been sent by the law to confirm the bandits' suspected presence at the Harless place, but he was obviously nervous and somewhat unconvincingly claimed that he was lost.

Mrs. Harless didn't believe him and the bandits took alarm, so much so that they posted Morris O'Malley as a sentry in a wagon near the barn. None of them saw the federal posse surrounding the house in the darkness. Deputy Marshals Tolbert and Ledbetter were out there in the night with five other men, simply biding their time until the house grew dark and quiet.

O'Malley wasn't much of a guard, for Bud Ledbetter appeared out of the gloom, threw down on Kelly, and left him bound and gagged in the barn. On the morning of November 30, Mrs. Harless's son appeared, walking out to fetch a bucket of water. He entered the barn and the officers snapped him up to join O'Malley. But when her son was missed around the family hearth, Mrs. Harless herself appeared and went into the barn. Ledbetter collared her and explained the situation.

He told her they had a warrant for Al Jennings, and he wanted her to go back inside and tell the outlaws they were surrounded. The outlaws were to come out with their hands up and surrender. If they didn't, she and her hired girl were to leave the house at once and go to the cemetery. Mrs. Harless returned to the house and delivered her message, and Ledbetter could hear sounds as of an argument from inside. Very quickly Mrs. Harless and the girl left the house, swathed in blankets against the cold.

Jennings opened fire on the lawmen, but this time he and his men were up against the first team. Within a few minutes it dawned on them that it was high time to leave. And so they did, running out the back of the cabin, heading for an orchard, and scrambling through fire from two possemen.

They were lucky, for one officer's rifle jammed at the first shot. A second got a charge of shot into Frank Jennings, without appreciably slowing him down. All of the bandits had been wounded, but none so crippled that they could not run at least a little way.

Al Jennings had been hit three times, including a bullet in his left thigh, but he could still move, and the bandits waded a creek and disappeared. Ledbetter was not happy, and he was even less so when the officers lost the trail and could not regain it after a long search. Taking Morris O'Malley and the gang's horses and horse furniture with them, the posse returned to Muskogee.

The fleeing gang members got a sort of transportation when they encountered two Indian boys in a wagon and commandeered both wagon and boys. The next day, after wandering somewhat aimlessly around the countryside, they stopped at the home of Willis Brooks. The gang may have been free, but they were in sad shape otherwise. Al and Pat O'Malley, at least, needed medical attention, and so they sent Brooks into town with directions to find a doctor.

Instead, he sought out and found Bud Ledbetter and told him where the gang was hiding. That night Ledbetter, Tolbert, and two other lawmen set up an ambush in a ravine where the road passed beneath high banks. They dropped a tree across the road as a barricade and settled in to wait.

They waited most of the night until a wagon came creaking out of the gloom with Al and Pat O'Malley bedded down in the back and Frank driving, following directions from Brooks that were supposed to take them to safety in Arkansas. In fact, Brooks had sent them straight into Ledbetter's trap. There was no fight this time. Confronted by four rifles, the outlaws gave it up and were transported to the Muskogee jail, where Morris O'Malley already languished.

Which left Little Dick West, still free, still wanted. West had friends in the Territory, so he could often find a safe place to hole up. Moreover, he had long been famous for wanting to sleep out of doors whatever the weather, someplace out in the brush away from people. He would be hard to catch.

But the law managed it, the law this time in the person of tough Deputy US Marshal Heck Thomas, who had kept order in the territory for many years, and who had killed Bill Doolin when the outlaw leader would not heed his order to surrender. If anybody could run West down, it would be Thomas.

West was now working as a farmhand between Kingfisher and Guthrie, laboring for two different farmers, Fitzgerald and Arnett. Mrs. Arnett spilled the beans when she was heard to say in Guthrie that Fitzgerald's hired hand was trying to get her husband to commit a robbery with him. Such evil tidings quickly found their way to Heck Thomas. The man had used an alias when he hired on, but Thomas guessed from the description that he was hearing about Little Dick West.

Accordingly, on the seventh of April, Thomas led a four-man posse, including the formidable Bill Tilghman, off to the Fitzgerald farm. Fitzgerald said he didn't know anything about the hired man, who in any event had long since left his employ. When the lawmen found a horse matching the description of West's in Fitzgerald's barn, the farmer said that he traded for the animal.

Unconvinced, the posse rode off toward the Arnett place, and on the way they got lucky, spotting a man "scouting along the timber to the left." Thomas and Tilghman began to follow him, and the others rode on toward Arnett's farm. There they saw the same man standing by a shed. The man promptly ran for it, and the three lawmen stepped into the open and ordered him to halt.

It was West, and his only response was to keep running and snap off several shots from his revolver. The lawmen responded with shotgun and rifle fire, and West was hit as he dove under the bottom strand of a barbed-wire fence. He was dead before the possemen could reach him.

Frank Jennings got five years hard time in Leavenworth; so did the O'Malleys. At that they were lucky, and Frank, at least, knew it. When he got out, Frank headed for the family home down in Oklahoma and passed from history.

There is a story that Temple Houston magnanimously offered to defend Al, an offer somewhat ungratefully refused. And so, in 1899 the court gave him a life term, but that dreadful sentence was later reduced to five years, allegedly through the able legal work of his brother John. He was out of durance vile in 1902 and received a presidential pardon five years later. Now he could start his second career, having been a notable failure at the first one.

Jennings settled in Oklahoma City in 1911, went back to practicing law, and almost immediately set his sights on political office. The next year he won nomination for county attorney of Oklahoma County on the Democratic ticket, but he lost in the general election. Nothing daunted, two years later he ran for governor, of all things, openly talking a lot about his outlaw days.

By then his life on the scout was commemorated not only by his 1913 book, *Beating Back*, but also by the film he made from the book, also called *Beating Back*. Al even starred in the movie, which at least gave him great face recognition with the voters.

It wasn't enough. The best Al could do was place third in a field of six in the Democratic primary. That was enough for him, so Al gave up both politics and the practice of law and retired to sunny California, where he went to work telling big lies, posing for innumerable swaggering "tough guy" photos, and working as an "advisor" to people making Western outlaw films. He worked hardest at assiduously cultivating his own myth as a real bad man.

Along the way he allowed as how he'd been a buddy of Jesse James—an interesting claim, since the Woodward gunfight with Houston had been in 1895 and Jesse was dead by early 1882. But at least Al was consistent about it: The moment he laid eyes on preposterous Jesse imposter J. Frank Dalton, he crowed that he knew that there feller was Jesse for sure.

Al died in Tarzana, California, the day after Christmas 1961. He had been a monumental flop as an outlaw, but all the same, it had been quite a life.

CHAPTER 19

Dirty Gold

The Reynolds Brothers

Outlaw brothers Jim and John Reynolds aren't names to conjure with, like Barker, or Dalton, or James, nor did Hollywood rush to make films about them and their escapades. But they were just as mean as their better-known brethren on the wrong side of the law, and as if to make up for that distinct character flaw and give something back to society, they left caches of loot here and there in Colorado. Or did they?

Lots of folks think they did, and for years people have been grubbing in the earth of Handcart Gulch and here and there and elsewhere, without, as far as anybody knows, finding anything worth taking with them. But the stories persist and maybe, just maybe, there's a small fortune waiting out there for some lucky digger. . . .

The Reynolds boys were Texans, born early in the nineteenth century. They had migrated to Colorado as early as 1862. They are said to have gone outlawing up in the South Park country, in company with three other Texas exports, men called McKee, Harrison, and Singleterry. Nobody caught them working, but they seemed always to have money in their jeans and good horses to ride. That was enough to make some people wonder about them, specifically whether they might just be the pests who had been robbing stages and the passengers who rode them. The robbers were masked of course, but the Reynolds' comfortable indolence did seem suspicious.

The citizens' assumptions were right for once, and things came to a head when the Reynolds gang took over a stage station called McLaughlin's, waited around until a stage came in, and absconded with the passengers' valuables and the mail sack. On the way they encountered a local business mogul named Major DeMary, a mine owner who local people said was known to stash his gold in anything, a tin, a pair of boots, a bucket. This meeting augured well for their big day, two birds with one stone.

There are at least two versions of what happened next, but at first, the great raid amounted to no more than a very small, disappointing payday; it was largely a fizzle.

The mine owner was also a bust. Either their victim wasn't packing gold that day, or he had it hidden where the gang couldn't find it. All they got was about a hundred dollars; split five ways that wasn't near enough to keep them in beans and 'baccy, and shoving DeMary around like bullies on a school ground soon lost their interest.

But the robbery at McLaughlin's was a much better payout. Their were no passengers on the stage, but the stage driver—who was also one of the owners—gave up about four hundred dollars and a gold watch while the strongbox yielded some three thousand dollars. The bandits ended their performance by stealing the coach's horses and chopping the spokes out of the vehicle's wheels, presumably to discourage pursuit, although chasing bandits in a stagecoach would seem to be an exercise in futility.

Their retreat seems to have been more a lark than a serious attempt to stay out of sight and unapprehended. At least, it was an outstanding example of bad bandit procedure. At one inn they stole more horses; at a second, they ate dinner and then robbed the woman who ran the place, until at last they reached Omaha House, a big building and well-known landmark.

The citizens of the nearby town of Fairplay raised a posse, which searched high and low until dark without finding a trace of their quarry. But the next day the gang fumbled their way back into prominence in the inimitable outlaw style. They rode up to a ranch and ordered the lady of the house to cook them a meal. The woman's husband, a man named Adolph Giraud, was apparently not watched carefully—or maybe not at all—and forthwith galloped into Fairplay. There a sizable posse saddled up and hurried off to Giraud's little ranch.

An alternative to the tale so far tells us that the gang was clanking with weaponry when they called at McLaughlin's, producing some uneasiness in the inhabitants. So much so that about the time the gang finished turning the coach wheels into kindling wood, a visiting man from a nearby town decided he had seen enough and rode for help.

This man, a Mr. Berry, followed the gang and tried to raise a posse to capture his quarry, then still loafing at the Omaha House. On his first try he could recruit no one, but he persisted and finally got a posse of one. With this puny force the intrepid man hied up to Omaha House and promptly got himself and his posseman captured.

The outlaws soon turned them loose, considering two unarmed citizens no threat, but they were, especially Berry. Once free, he galloped cross-country spreading the word of the Texas invasion, rather like Paul Revere stirring up "every Middlesex village and farm" in the famous poem by Henry Wadsworth Longfellow. Sure enough, the five cocky outlaws were still dawdling over dinner when the posse showed up and packed them off to jail in Denver. The Fairplay citizens had done their job, but the Denver jailer did not. For by the next evening

the Reynolds boys and their three hoodlum buddies had escaped, pur-
loined some likely looking horseflesh, and vanished, supposedly back
to Texas. In any case, they were seen no more for a while.

Now the year was 1864, and the Civil War was raging; Gettysburg
had been fought, but Appomattox was still a very long way ahead. The
Confederacy, cut off from foreign markets for its cotton, was already
feeling the pinch. Real money was getting scarcer and scarcer, and Jim
Reynolds had the answer . . . or he said he did, and his grand plan was
this.

He would recruit a guerrilla force and return to Colorado, there
to capture all that gold. He would then haul it back into the Confederacy, and the question of war finance would be solved. He announced,
moreover, that his offer had been accepted by the Confederate government. His fanciful offer may have been made, but it would probably
have been rejected. It is equally possible that his "gold mission" was no
more than an invention, raised to support his monstrous ego and give
him, his brother, and whomever else he could find to ride along a sort
of quasi-military status.

That status could be important in the fog of guerrilla war, and
it might even save him or his brother John or their followers from
ending their career suddenly and without due process of law, abruptly
dangled from a handy tree. Citizens could get a little precipitate when
their relatives and neighbors were being victimized.

In aid of creating a new *persona* and further inflating his sense
of self-worth, Jim reinvented himself as a CSA officer, a colonel, no
less; no working up through the ranks for him. Predictably, there is no
record that he ever held that formidable rank or indeed that he was
commissioned, or for that matter that he spent any time in Confederate gray at all.

Jim did return to Colorado at least, with an "army" of just a few
men, probably no more than twenty-three. Most of them were the
trash of the territory; a lot of his recruiting had been done in and

around Las Vegas, New Mexico, later to be the stomping ground of such murderous thugs as HooDoo Brown, Dirty Dave Rudabaugh, and Mysterious Dave Mather.

But for a while things went smooth as a baby's bottom. The first strike was the interception of a wagon train coming to Santa Fe out of Chihuahua. Some sixty thousand dollars in minted gold was the haul from that one, and the gang got away unscathed into the Sangre de Cristo Mountains. The plan, one account tells, was to bury this lovely loot, and then, after the gang added to it from other strikes, haul the whole pile back to Texas to help out the war effort.

Whether that whole idea was moonshine or not, it didn't happen. A good many of the Reynolds' dubious Las Vegas recruits wanted their cut of the booty and they wanted it *now*. Reynolds agreed—he may not have had a choice—and the majority of his "soldiers" took their gold and skedaddled. That reduced the gang to just nine, and that included the two Reynolds brothers and only one of their original gang, Owen Singleterry.

So the sadly reduced army went on to the South Park country, somewhere over the headwaters of the South Platte River, leaving, legend tells us, their shares of the golden hoard buried somewhere in the Sangre de Cristos. That lost gold is still there, as far as anybody knows, if indeed it ever was. At least, if anybody stumbled across it, they didn't talk about it.

For a while, things went well for the gang in their new lair, and their stage holdups went pretty much as planned. Posses chasing them came up empty repeatedly, maybe in part because Reynolds seems to have had some helpers among the small ranchers in the area, serving as his intelligence service either out of fear or the sunshine a little gold brought into their hardscrabble lives.

Still, for Jim and John and the hard-core warriors who had stuck with them, the booty from their repeated little holdups didn't satisfy their craving for the big time. After all, if you held up a stage, you might get a thousand dollars on a good day, and there were eight mouths and egos to feed.

And so Jim called a council of war, and the boys talked it over. They needed to go on to greater things, and for Jim that greater thing was nothing less than a raid on the Territorial Treasury itself. Everybody bought into this ambitious enterprise, and so the boys headed for Denver, where their bonanza awaited. Along the way they stopped to eat at the Omaha House and ran off at the mouth—it seems these boys were given to doing something inane over dinner.

And so it was. They were overheard, and the man who listened to them babble galloped through the night to warn Denver's finest. A doughty police captain named Maynard raised a large posse and moved to intercept the outlaws. In those days, there was a good deal less of the "Halt, Police!" stuff, and more of Texas John Slaughter's "shoot first and shout 'Throw up your hands!' after," and so it was with Maynard and his boys. They simply charged the Reynolds gang and won the resulting gunfight. The outlaws, several of them wounded, turned tail and stood not upon the order of their going.

Back in cover in South Park, the gang took a month or so off. The wounded—one was Singleterry—had time to recover, and the Reynolds boys could dream up more ambitions plans. Then it was time again for productive operations, and this time the gang again chose nearby Fairplay and McLaughlin's stage depot. They knew the country, and, after all, it was close to their hideout.

For some reason gold had accumulated in Fairplay, and so there was a good deal of it on board this stage. Nobody knows for sure just how much, but one estimate puts the value at about sixty thousand dollars. As they had before, the Reynolds boys seized the station and when the McClellen and Spottswood stage rolled in, passengers and driver—he was one of the stage line's owners—were helpless.

This robbery was a mighty good day in terms of loot, but it proved to be the straw that broke the camel's back with the area's residents.

Multiple posses took the field and kept the gang on the move. And a member of one of these, investigating a distant campfire, discovered that it was not another posse as he first thought, but their quarry instead. Or maybe, in the alternative version, a soldier of the pursuing cavalry had fallen behind his unit and was around Slaghts Freight Station when the gang showed up. He rode for help, but the outlaws were gone by the time reinforcements arrived.

But that was the last luck the outlaws had, the last good luck, anyway. With multiple posses on their back trail, they found an enemy in their way no matter how they twisted and turned. And at last one posse spotted the outlaw fire, and the firefight followed.

Singleterry was killed, the gang ran for their lives, and five more of them were captured, including the great woolly ram, Jim Reynolds. Only three bandits, led by John Reynolds, got away.

The gang still had some bad luck coming. After a one-night stand in a Denver jail, the prisoners were to be taken to Fort Wise and delivered to the US Army there, classified as regular enemy combatants. There seems to have been no evidence on which to base this finding, except the assertions of the prisoners, or of some of them. And in all probability, this story was a total sham.

According to more reliable sources, the five prisoners were collected from the Denver jail by a Captain Cree, leading a detachment of the Third Colorado Cavalry. Cree and his men duly returned to Denver with the sad news that all five had been killed while attempting to escape.

That story gets a little hard to believe if in fact another story is true: A scout found all five bodies tied to trees and full of bullets. So much for due process of law, but at least there was no chance of hung juries or appeals or similar inconvenience.

The *Rocky Mountain News* told the story another way. Reynolds boasted of his exploits and said that "he had intended to destroy Denver and that he expected yet to lay the city in ashes." He also talked about emulating the vile Quantrill, and his men were "abusive and insolent," to the point that Cree warned his prisoners that his men were so angry that Cree could barely control them.

In any case, said the *News*, "Few will regret their end and many will breathe easier that they are gone." Which was a dignified way of saying, "Who cares? Good riddance."

On that note—murder or attempted escape—the story ends, except for the gold. For John Reynolds later returned to Colorado, and the probabilities are that he would have lost no time in retrieving the gang's fabulous stash. He certainly headed back to that very part of the country where you might expect to find it hidden: Reynolds was in South Park in 1871. He and a partner were busy stealing horses there and got themselves killed.

But well, maybe he hadn't dug all that loot up before he was killed. So maybe the stolen gold is out there in the mountains yet. Lots of treasure hunters have thought so, and even myths die hard.

Neither John Reynolds nor his brother is talking.

CHAPTER 20

Revenge

The McCluskies

There were family groups that stayed on the right side of the law, as well as those who broke it. Notable examples are the Masterson boys, Bat, Ed, and Jim, all of them pillars of the law, but they don't make this book because they were among the Good Guys. But an exception is made to tell the remarkable tale of the McCluskie boys.

They weren't outlaws as far as history records; bad blood was not apparent in their lives, although they were no strangers to violence, and there is evidence that McCluskie was not the name with which they started life. But they find a place here because of their courage and fighting ability, their fierce brotherly loyalty to each other, and, in particular, the way their story ends.

Back in 1871, the town of Newton, Kansas, could safely be called hell on wheels. Newton wasn't much of a place by eastern standards, but in that far-off year it had a certain importance it would never know again. For Newton sat along the Atchison, Topeka and Santa Fe Railway, and it was then the northern terminus of the Chisholm Trail. Up that trail came the great herds of Texas beef bound for the eastern markets, and with the herds came the cowboys.

The cowboys were Texans, mostly. Wherever they came from, most of them were wild youngsters, tough, wiry, and full of vinegar. By the time they finished a drive, they had been forty to seventy days on the trail. They had braved stampedes, rustlers, bad water, worse food, and weeks of sweat-soaked, saddle-sore riding to bring the great herds to the railhead. They were ready for some fun, and they had money in their jeans.

Now fun, after the obligatory bath, haircut, and restaurant meal—and sometimes before these things—meant booze, women, and gambling, and lots of at least the first two. Like the other wild Kansas railhead towns, Abilene, Caldwell, Dodge City, and the rest, Newton in its heyday attracted swarms of both amateur and professional whores, cardsharps, booze peddlers, feather merchants, and an assortment of just plain hoodlums.

Stirring all these transient predators together with a flock of tough Texans was a sure recipe for big trouble. The cowboys went armed as a matter of course, and so did the bar owners and the gamblers and the pimps ("blacksmith" was a favorite euphemism for this ancient and unpleasant trade, as in "he blacksmithed for Sadie"). In spite of ordinances that prohibited carrying sidearms within the city limits, the cow towns saw a lot of quarrels settled abruptly in a whiff of gunpowder smoke. So it was in Newton.

The railroad came to Newton in July 1871. The Santa Fe line was built to cut off rival Kansas Pacific's beef terminus in Abilene, to the north. Newton boasted about fifteen hundred inhabitants in that year, together with a cluster of raw wood buildings and some tents. The first building—a blacksmith shop—was completed only in mid-April, but by late summer the town comprised about two hundred structures of one kind or another. The main street was either glutinous, bottomless bog or unyielding hardpan, depending on the weather.

The "pleasure section" of the town, down in its southeast corner, was called "Hide Park," although whether the reference was to skin bovine, or human, or both, is now lost in the mist of time. You could buy firewater in twenty-seven different establishments, large and small. The Gold Room was Newton's swank watering hole, but you could drown your sorrows in the Bull's Head and the Lone Star, too, and a couple of dozen other places.

In any case, Newton quickly won the unenviable title of "the wickedest town in Kansas," which, as one Kansan neatly put it, "was going some, for Kansas in the past has had some towns that in a competitive examination for wickedness would give hell a neck and neck race."

Newton would not even be formally incorporated until the early part of 1872, when Harvey County was also created. Just now, in the summer of 1871, it may not have been formally a city, but it sure was busy.

Hide Park's chief emporia were two big dance halls, separated by about thirty yards. Ed Krum owned one, the Alamo. Tuttle's Dance Hall, owned by Perry Tuttle, was the other. There were other buildings close by from which the local soiled doves also plied their ancient profession. Since Hide Park was never an oasis of peace, the town had hired an enforcer, a husky quasi lawman named Mike McCluskie. He was appointed the "night policeman," and to him fell the herculean task of keeping whatever passed for order in Hide Park.

McCluskie was not the name by which Mike's mother would have known him, for he'd begun life as Arthur Delaney (or maybe it was Donovan). Since many of the cow town denizens had experienced trouble elsewhere, bogus identities were not uncommon. Indeed, a fresh name was often downright essential to any kind of comfortable survival. So it was with McCluskie, who, it was said, had departed his native Missouri in unseemly haste. By trade he was an ironfisted railroad section boss, and he was a tough customer by anybody's definition.

The trouble began on the eleventh of August 1871, a Friday. The city was voting on a bond proposal, and the polls were protected by a special policeman hired for the day, a Texan by the name of William Bailey. Bailey—or Baylor, his real name—had something of a reputation, having killed a couple of men someplace in Texas, and he was pushy and unpleasant.

Bailey was, as one commentator put it, "the very worst choice for such duty. As a peace officer, he was no more than a very dangerous clown with a badge."

To make matters worse, Bailey had spent election morning getting soused, and in the afternoon he began to harass the election officials. They called in McCluskie, who had struck sparks with Bailey before this.

McCluskie dealt with the drunken Bailey somewhat summarily. He simply yanked him out on the street, where he called Bailey every dirty name in the book, astonishing even the tough citizens of Newton with his eloquence.

It was not the kind of humiliation a Texas bad man could stomach.

And so that evening Bailey, still quite drunk or maybe more so, found McCluskie in front of the Red Front saloon and demanded McCluskie buy drinks for the large crowd present. McCluskie, of course, was having none of that. The argument moved inside the saloon, and, one thing leading to another, Bailey rashly attacked big McCluskie with his fists. That turned out to be unwise, for McCluskie smote Bailey mightily in the forehead with his fist, sending him reeling through the saloon doors into the street.

McCluskie followed his foe into the dusty street and found Bailey leaning against a hitching post, clutching a revolver. McCluskie dug for his own weapon and fired twice, Bailey went down with a bullet under the heart, and the fight was over. Bailey lingered until the morning, and thereafter was duly transported to Newton's Boot Hill.

That should have been the end of the fight, but it wasn't. In the nature of things on the frontier, a man's friends were inclined to take up his quarrels and carry them on. So it was in this case. For although McCluskie thoughtfully departed on the morning train to let Newton cool off, some of Bailey's Texan friends brooded together and swore vengeance.

And so, when McCluskie returned to Newton, there was big trouble waiting for him. Most of it came from a group of cowboys led by one Hugh Anderson, a wild youngster who had recently come to Newton with his father's Texas herd. Anderson had something of a reputation himself, earned in a couple of shooting scrapes back in Bell County, Texas.

McCluskie, apparently unaware of his mortal danger, or just uncaring, returned to town on Saturday and that evening betook himself to Perry Tuttle's to drink and gamble. He sat happily at a corner table and did not seem worried, even though several friends had warned him that the Texans were out to kill him. Tuttle knew trouble was on the way. At one point he even tried to close his doors to head it off, but the patrons roared their disapproval. Even after he sent his band home, the place remained full and booming.

McCluskie continued to act unconcerned when several Texans approached his table and one of them even sat down to talk to him. What McCluskie did not know was that the Texans had sent for Anderson and now were simply waiting for the fireworks.

They did not have long. A little past midnight, Anderson bulled up to McCluskie's table, his revolver already in his fist, and the Texan supporting players moved back to give Anderson room. "You are a cowardly son-of-a-bitch!" roared Anderson. "I'll blow the top of your head off!"

Suiting the action to the word, Anderson blazed away. Though he may have aimed at McCluskie's head, his slug slammed into McCluskie's neck. Game to the end, blood pouring from his throat,

McCluskie stood up, jerked out his Colt, leveled it, pulled the trigger . . . and the weapon misfired.

Anderson fired again, hitting McCluskie in the leg and knocking him down. McCluskie got his six-gun to working now, but he was apparently too badly hurt to hit his foe even at this point-blank range. Anderson kept on firing, hitting McCluskie again in the body. About this time shooting became general in Tuttle's, although the exact sequence of events has vanished forever in the powder smoke. Several patrons had pulled their revolvers, and men began to fall.

Now enters another leading player in the fight at Tuttle's. He was an unlikely desperado, a sickly, slim waif of about eighteen years of age named Jim Riley. One Harvey County judge called Riley "quiet and inoffensive in deportment," and so he had been . . . until that night. Riley had wandered into Newton from who knew where, broke and coughing badly from tuberculosis, and McCluskie had sheltered him, fed him, and befriended him. Now Riley saw his friend and benefactor bleeding on the saloon floor.

Riley calmly turned and locked the saloon door and then pulled his revolver and went to killing. Since a good many folks were banging away in various directions, nobody ever knew for sure exactly who shot whom when, but it is certain that Riley was absolutely intent on ventilating the man who had downed McCluskie.

And when the smoke at last blew away, Perry Tuttle's place was a shambles. Anderson was down with two wicked leg wounds. A cowboy by the name of Martin was bleeding to death from a throat wound. Two railroad men, Lee and Hickey, had been badly wounded; Lee, shot in the gut, would not survive. Scattered across the blood-splattered saloon floor were cowboys Billy Garrett and Henry Kearnes, dying of bullets in the throat and chest. Two other cowboys were wounded.

Not long after the sun came up that Sunday morning, the city held an inquest. Riley had sensibly departed Newton for more congenial climes, but a warrant was issued for Anderson after McCluskie died about eight o'clock, although it was not served because of the young Texan's perilous condition. But Anderson's father had already schemed to protect his vicious son, worried not only about his two severe wounds but also about the townsmen's talk of a summary necktie party.

Anderson Sr. arranged with the worried city fathers of Newton to smuggle his wastrel offspring out of town by railroad, concealed in the closet of a passenger car. The Texans successfully got Anderson aboard the train in the darkness before dawn and safely through to sophisticated medical treatment in Kansas City. The doctors saved his life, but he did not keep it long, as we shall see.

Nobody knows what happened to Riley. A headline in the Topeka *Kansas Daily Commonwealth* said simply "The Desperadoes 'Vamoosed,'" without elaboration. One story has Riley dying of his tuberculosis in Colorado—shades of Doc Holliday. Another says he was killed out west, in New Mexico or Arizona. Whatever happened to the deadly young man, his disappearance and Anderson's serious wounds and flight should have ended the saga of Tuttle's Dance Hall.

But they didn't.

One version of the end of this story, a relatively tame one, says only that Anderson, crippled by his Newton wounds, died in Texas a few years after the fight. However, there is also another, much more lurid and far more satisfying finale to the saga of the great Newton gunfight.

The story of the second ending is said to have appeared in the Reading, Pennsylvania, newspaper *Gazette and Democrat* on August 2, 1873. The writer is supposed to have been a "correspondent of the *New York World*," who wrote the tale from Medicine Lodge, Kansas. Precisely why the *World* would have a correspondent in benighted little Medicine Lodge, and how the *Gazette and Democrat* came by the story, are lost in the mists of the past.

Nevertheless, the account did describe Medicine Lodge much as it was in those days, so maybe the story is actually true. True or not, it is dandy melodrama, infinitely more interesting than the tame version that has Hugh Anderson dying in bed in Texas. Here it is.

This last act was not written until two summers later, and it was played out in Medicine Lodge, which was only a wide spot in the trail in those days. There were a couple of "good-sized buildings used for storage," but otherwise the settlement boasted only five houses, a hotel of sorts, and a two-room log trading post that doubled as a saloon.

In June of 1873, into tiny Medicine Lodge rode another McCluskie, a big, husky brother called Arthur. He was "a handsome brute in a buckskin suit," and he announced that he was looking for Hugh Anderson. Anderson was in town all right, tending bar, and McCluskie lost no time in sending in a semiformal choose-your-own-weapons challenge to mortal combat.

Anderson chose pistols, being somewhat smaller than his challenger, and maybe remembering what happened to Bailey when he closed with Mike McCluskie back in Newton. Anyhow, the two men arranged to duel in the grand old style, standing twenty paces apart with their backs turned. They would then whirl to confront each other, signaled by a shot fired by a huge, bearded gent called Harding, owner of the trading-post-cum-bar and Anderson's boss.

Not much exciting was wont to happen in minuscule Medicine Lodge, and so the duel drew a crowd—perhaps seventy men were on hand to watch the bloodshed, and that was surely a multitude for the town. There was some betting by the spectators and general hopeful expectation of a really entertaining fight. In the event, nobody was going to be disappointed.

It is hard to imagine two experienced frontiersmen missing each other at twenty paces, but that is exactly what they did. With his second shot, however, McCluskie broke Anderson's left arm. As he went down, Anderson drove a slug through McCluskie's mouth, and McCluskie rushed him, spewing out blood and teeth and working his pistol. Anderson kept shooting back, coolly hitting McCluskie again and again, until the big man's legs would no longer hold him up.

Both men were running out of ammunition now, but neither one would quit. Some of the bystanders, appalled by the blood and the pit bull spirit of the fighters, began to call for an end to the fight. Harding would not stop it, however. The terms had been a fight to the death—both men had agreed, and that was that. And so it went on.

On the ground, body torn with bullets but still game, McCluskie nailed Anderson with a bullet in the belly. The impact of the slug, probably McCluskie's last round, knocked the Texan on his back. Now McCluskie, knife in hand, began to drag himself across the ground toward his foe, leaving a trail of blood as he crawled. As he reached Anderson, the blood-splashed Texan made one last effort, heaving himself to a sitting position and slashing McCluskie's throat with his knife. McCluskie sank his own blade into Anderson's side, and both men collapsed in the dust.

The fight was finished, and so were both fighters. There was nothing left now but to bury what remained of the contestants, and that solemn task was duly attended to. Both men were unceremoniously wrapped in hides and trucked off to an unmarked common grave; as far as anybody knows, they are there yet, waiting together for the last trumpet. They did have a memorial of sorts, a ballad by poet Richard Wheeler, which goes in part like this:

> There's a spot in the town of Medicine Lodge,
> Where a pair who fought till they died,
> Have been laid away
> Till the Judgment Day
> And are waiting it side by side.

CHAPTER 21

Late Beginners

Rube and Jim Burrow

Rueben Burrow (sometimes Burrows) started his criminal career later than the average outlaw. Most of the punks who set out to rob and kill people for fun and profit were youngsters, but Rube was thirty-two when he went bad in 1886, a comparative Methuselah for his time.

He had started out on the right side of the law when he ranched in Arkansas and later when he moved to a property near Stephenville, Texas. He married, had two children, and was a well-respected citizen, a Mason in the local lodge.

His wife died after just four years of marriage, but Rube raised the little ones alone until he married again four years later. About that time he bought a farm near the hamlet of Alexander, Texas, and set out to peacefully farm. His luck was not in, however, and after his crops failed, he looked around for a more reliable way of making his way in the world.

The solution was, he concluded, train robbery. After all, the iron horse regularly carried lots of desirable things, real money and sometimes gold bullion in the express car, registered letters in the mail car, and passengers with pockets that jingled. And trains regularly ran to the same places at the same times; they could not escape you by turning aside and dashing for some safe place.

So Rube raised his own little gang, with his younger brother Jim as the nucleus. He added a couple of no-goods named Brock—also brothers—and on the first of December, 1886, they stopped a Fort Worth and Denver train, robbing the passengers of their valuables but skipping the mail car, which for some reason they thought was heavily guarded. Part of their loot included the weapons of a squad of soldiers the gang found sound asleep in the last car.

The take was only a few hundred dollars, and so, when they stopped their next train—a Texas and Pacific passenger train—on January 23, 1887, they took on the mail car as well. It proved to be a piece of cake. Herding the engine crew before him, Rube commanded the mail messenger to open up, and when that courageous man refused, Rube fired several times in the air and loudly announced that he had dispatched the engineer and fireman. Open the door, he commanded, or I'll start on the passengers.

At this the car door opened, and the gang got more than two thousand dollars. That was a lot of money in 1887, and it whetted the gang's appetite for more . . . much more. And so, in June, Rube and Jim and their henchmen hit another Texas and Pacific train and did even better: three thousand dollars this time.

That holdup had worked so well that in September they stuck up another Texas and Pacific train. In fact, it was the same train, with the same crew, at the same place. The take was about the same as the last time, and then they got another thirty-five hundred dollars from robbing the St. Louis, Arkansas and Texas train up in Arkansas. This time, however, they narrowly missed being captured by the local sheriff.

But they kept it up, until the railroads began to wonder if the gang was getting inside information from somebody with knowledge of the railroad network. For the gang got another three thousand dollars or so from a Fort Worth and Denver train in early 1888, and they hit the poor old Texas and Pacific again for another couple of thousand.

But this time the railroad detectives had something to go on, for one of the Brock brothers had left behind a new raincoat. It was traced back to him, and on his confession he was sent away to think about his sins for the next twenty years. He didn't begin to make it, preferring to hurl himself from a four-story cell tier.

Pinkerton detectives were by now hot on the trail of the gang, entering the front door of Burrow's family home in Alabama as Jim ran out the back door. The railroads now took the intelligent step of providing all conductors with sketches and descriptions of the gang, a tactic that soon bore fruit.

Jim and Rube barely escaped capture when a conductor recognized them and called police; fleeing down a street from the railroad station, they were spotted by a reporter, who also shouted for police until Jim shot him down. Their bad luck was just beginning, for a short time later they were spotted at a Nashville station. Rube shot his way clear, but Jim was captured. He was a nasty prisoner, bragging about all the crimes he and Rube had committed and delivering this arrogant message: "My name is Jim Burrow, and the other man on the train is my brother Rube, and if you give us two pistols apiece, we are not afraid of any two men living."

Maybe so, but there was something he should have feared. For before the year was out, Jim Burrow was dead of tuberculosis.

Rube, now alone, became increasingly vicious. During the holdup of a train in December of 1888 he murdered an Illinois Central passenger who didn't want to give up his wallet.

And the following June, it got even worse. Rube asked a relative to pick up a package for him at the local post office, and the postmaster refused to let the relative sign for the mail. Rube went to town and shot the postmaster down in front of his wife. Tipping his hat, the story goes, he rode out of town.

In spite of his vicious nature, Rube was pretty well protected on his run-down farm in Lamar County, Alabama, where he had built a secret room in his house, complete with concealed firing ports. Kinfolk and friends would warn him if there were lawmen about. Rube wasn't bright enough to stop robbing, however, and with a new henchman, one Jackson, he hit a train at Buckatunna, Alabama, getting away with a real bonanza for the time, around eleven thousand dollars.

A plague of other train holdups followed, although Rube probably didn't commit all that were attributed to him. At least one man ended up dead after being mistaken for Rube, a cousin who was shot down for the seventy-five-hundred-dollar reward on Rube's head. Jackson was captured by the authorities, but Rube managed at least one more train robbery before his time came. This time it was the Louisville and Nashville, poorer by some four thousand dollars, in mid-1890.

It was Rube's last hurrah. He went shopping in Linden, Alabama, perusing the local hardware store for rifles. Carter, the clerk, alertly went into the back room, checked some wanted posters, and emerged with his own rifle. He locked Rube in the storeroom and went off to find some law, but while he was away, Rube broke out.

Now, most men would, in the language of the day, have "taken it on the heel and toe"; not Rube. He was, the story goes, humiliated by being captured by a lowly store clerk; the cure for his unhappiness was to seek out the clerk to kill him. It was a big mistake, a terminal one.

For when he caught up with Carter and opened up on him, Carter pulled his own pistol and returned fire; both men fought it out in the street. Rube drew first blood, hitting Carter in the arm. But Carter's aim was better, and his retort ripped open Burrow's stomach. He died in the street, but Carter would survive to receive the reward.

What remained of Rube was shipped home, where he was met by an assortment of people, including his mother and father. One last humiliation awaited: When he was unloaded from the baggage car, he came flying out of his coffin, thrown, one tale says, by detectives accompanying the remains. The outlaw's corpse was allegedly covered with an assortment of terrible scars, the products of some postmortem kicking around by lawmen.

Maybe so, maybe not, but it's hard to get too excited over the indignity when you remember the postmaster who was spitefully murdered in front of his wife.

CHAPTER 22

Just Down-Home Folks

The Newton Boys

Willis Newton characterized the Newton boys' career a trifle more sanctimoniously than he should have when he said, "Bonnie and Clyde was just silly kids . . . we wasn't at all like them . . . all we wanted was the money, just like . . . other businessmen."

Well, not quite like other businessmen, for the Newton boys used guns and nitroglycerin as their primary tools instead of law books or scalpels or adding machines. But at least they generally behaved fairly reasonably, if you didn't mind getting robbed all that much. They were certainly not psychopathic scum like Larry DeVol or his ilk.

And indeed, the Newtons became pretty good at their "business," leading Willis Newton to brag a little later on: "In my time I robbed over eighty banks and six trains. . . . I don't want to say how much money it all added up to, but it was more than Jesse James, the Dalton boys, and Bonnie and Clyde got, all put together."

Maybe so.

There were four Newton brothers, which most bankers thought was about four too many. But in fact, if you had to be held up by somebody, the Newton brothers would probably be your first choice. They were even pleasant, often passing the time of day with their victims . . . while they stole their worldly goods.

They were named Willis, Joe, Jess, and Dock. They were Texas boys, out of Uvalde, part of a family of eleven kids. Still in their teens, Dock and Willis got two years for stealing cotton in 1910. Dock, ever the man of action of the boys, spent his time up the river thinking up various ways to escape—none of them bore fruit—until at last the boys' long-suffering mother pleaded with the governor to at least let the more peaceful Willis out early, so that he could help with the miserable task of picking cotton on the old home place.

By the end of 1914, Willis decided he wasn't cut out for the peaceful bucolic life, and he went off with a friend to hold up a train and rob its passengers of their worldly goods, almost five Gs' worth. He got away with that one, but he also went on dabbling in penny-ante crime and got caught peddling, of all things, a pile of pilfered clothing. That got him two more years in jail.

But now Willis showed a flash of real genius: He wrote the judge who sentenced him and the lawman who nabbed him and asked each of them to sign a petition for his parole. They wrote in reply, and their response was no surprise: not no, but hell no. But their mercy was not what Willis was looking for: All he really wanted was their signatures, and once he had those, he forged them onto his own petition. It worked.

Back to the big time. From here on, no more lifting long johns. From here on it would be banks; Willis had discovered the eternal truth that Willie Sutton put so well: "That's where the money is." He is said to have rationalized his decision in the time-tested way: "Some of them banks out in West Texas didn't care about hurtin' us poor farmers, so why would I care about hurtin' them?"

This was long before the advent of the FDIC, so those same poor farmers were unprotected if the bank went belly up unless it carried private insurance. Maybe Willis didn't know that, but if he did think of it, his expressed pious sympathy for his fellow farmers didn't get between him and their money.

Willis figured he would need help robbing banks, and brothers Dock—just escaped from jail—young Joe, and Jess were willing. Just about anything beat picking cotton in the blazing sun, and the lure of lots of money was a potent siren to poor farm boys and ex-jailbirds.

The Newtons started off with nighttime raids, hitting country banks especially during autumn harvest time, when farmers deposited their earnings. The boys became artists with nitroglycerin; as Willis reasonably commented, "That's what it's made for, is to blow banks." So for a while the gang concentrated on smaller targets, using nitro—"grease" to the outlaw fraternity—and they became experts on which kind of safe the stuff worked on the best.

The safe door had to have right-angle doors; that way, the nitro lodged nicely in the cracks between the doors and the safe itself. Round doors were to be avoided: The nitro ran out before you could fire it, or if it did go off, there wasn't enough left to bust the door.

They traveled around, spreading their handiwork on square doors from Texas to Canada and points in between. It worked, and the poor country boys had money to spend, until at last they got greedy and decided to go for a daylight robbery. Willis seems to have been the mastermind of this one, flying in the face of his own maxim: It was better to say "there he goes," rather than "here he lies."

He should have listened to himself.

The boys picked a bank in New Braunfels, Texas, in 1923, and it turned out to be a bonanza: just over one hundred thousand dollars. That sure beat stealing other people's pants and even nighttime blasts of unstable grease.

There were risks, of course. Among other things, the Texas Bankers Association posted an announcement in all of its banks. Its intent was crystal clear: "Reward. Five thousand dollars for dead bank robbers. Not one cent for live ones."

If that terse announcement seemed a little short on notions of due process of law, in practice it made eminent good sense. Like lynching, it eliminated the chance of such inconveniences as hung juries, appeals, mistrials, and such.

Then there was the Toronto robbery in 1923, an unusual raid because the gang attacked a currency clearinghouse rather than a bank. In those days the banks—at least the major ones—had currency of their own. They took in money during the day, and at night it was loaded into trucks and taken to the clearinghouse to be sorted out. Then next business morning, each bank got its own currency back. Couriers carried big bags of money out of each bank each night and carried bags back to the banks the next morning.

The sight of all those bags of money made the gang's mouths water. They did their usual careful reconnaissance, but they didn't account for the confusion of crowded streets and courageous couriers who wouldn't give up the sacks they carried. Willis wounded a bank guard who intervened to try to help the couriers and was shooting at the robbers from the window of his automobile.

Couriers scattered in all directions. The outlaws got two sacks, but then they had to run for their lives. People in the surrounding buildings were throwing chairs and anything else they could lift down at the robbers, and the police were closing in; the gang had to do some fancy driving through traffic to get clear. The car was quickly hidden in a garage, and Willis and Dock took themselves out of the line of fire by going to a movie.

Willis said later that he was concerned for anybody that might get in the gang's way. "I always told the boys, 'If you have to shoot don't shoot to kill.'" Which sounded good after the fact but apparently didn't consider the difficulty involved in just nicking somebody in the midst of a multigun melee. He also said the gang "loaded our guns with birdshot a lot of times just so we wouldn't kill anybody."

The tremendous New Braunfels and Toronto successes whetted the gang's collective appetite for still bigger and better things. Especially Willis's ambition now knew no bounds, and that led him to rob a train in the summer of 1924 on a tip that it was loaded with money and diamonds. Young Joe had his doubts about this undertaking, but Willis was the boss, and he made the call to take down the train at a town called Roundout, some thirty miles from Chicago.

It turned out to be the biggest train holdup in American history, eclipsing all the raids more famous outlaws had made before. The gang apparently did have inside information, supposedly from somebody in the postal service and from a "high-placed" Chicago politician. The target was a Chicago, Milwaukee and St. Paul mail train, and they struck it only twenty-five miles or so from Chicago. This time Willis took along some extra help, a confederate named Brent Glasscock, who had worked with the Newtons before.

The gang had watched carefully as mail trucks rolled one after another into the train depot. It was tempting to rob one or more trucks as they arrived, but the police station was only a couple of blocks away; if they robbed the trucks "right here on the street, we was liable to have to shoot somebody." So the plan shifted gears: Let all that money get out of town, together in one place, and take it there. While they were waiting and planning, they struck a payroll out in Cicero for a cool thirty-five thousand dollars.

The train remained the big goal, however, the golden fleece, the bonanza. The plan to take it was carefully worked out since the target was the sacks of registered mail. There was the question of whether to use gas on the mail clerks or go in without it, how to get away with multiple heavy mailbags, and planning for the all-important getaway. Their careful preparation included stealing a couple of cars—both

Cadillacs—fueling them, and then stashing them in rented garages until the gang was ready to move.

Their careful preparation paid off to a point; two of the gang got on the train, thoughtfully wearing overalls and caps, booted several hobos off the train, moved in on the engineer and fireman and ordered them to stop the train. And they got it stopped, although the engineer, understandably frightened, overshot the gang's appointed stopping place at Roundout by a whole train length.

The mail clerks were forced to open the car door with a threat of poison gas—in fact a bottle of formaldehyde—and came out, a total according to the outlaws of "seventeen," leaving their revolvers in the car, and were set to work loading the stolen mailbags in the bandits' Cadillacs . . . and that was when the whole operation came unstuck.

For Glasscock, for reasons not apparent then or later, started shooting. It wasn't a clerk he hit, although that would have been bad enough, it was Dock Newton, hit several times, and "bleeding like a stuck hog."

The gang managed to get clear of the holdup site and discovered they had hit the proverbial jackpot, some three million dollars in cash and bonds, a haul that could have, in Willis's words, financed a trip to Mexico "where we could buy ourselves some ranch land and live like kings." But there was Dock, in bad shape from Glasscock's panicked shooting, and he had to be helped first. A doctor's visit was arranged, but somebody had seen the rest of the gang carry a man in a chair into the apartment where they hid out. And so the boys passed into captivity.

The later years were kind to the brothers. On sentencing they managed a sweetheart deal, negotiating remarkably light sentences in return for turning over most of the loot. Joe got only a year in Leavenworth, and the other brothers were free men by 1929.

The gang was never reformed. Jess worked on ranches in Texas until cancer got him in 1960. Joe returned to Texas, where he operated a couple of businesses and farmed with his father for a while. Dock got involved in still another burglary—a store, this time. He spent eight months in the prison hospital for what Willis wrote later was a frame-up. He passed away in 1974, also of cancer.

Willis and Joe lived on, enjoying their mutual hobby of beekeeping. Willis died in 1979, and Joe lasted a decade longer. Willis, the leader of the pack, retained his professional pride, looking down on people in the robbery business he considered his inferiors. Bonnie and Clyde, for instance, "never robbed a bank in their life, they just robbed filling stations and stores." The brothers' outlaw successes put them, in Willis's eyes, far above all the other hoodlums who would have loved to rob other people but "just didn't have the guts . . . they wouldn't have known how to do it. They couldn't rob a kitchen safe."

CHAPTER 23

A Flash in the Pan

The Poe-Hart Gang

Very few people these days have even heard of the Poe-Hart gang; anybody who reads about their time is generally interested in the big names: the Daltons, Bonnie and Clyde, Pretty Boy Floyd, the noxious Barker family. The Poe-Hart bunch didn't last very long, and they were a far cry from romantic, but while they were on the prowl they were hell on wheels to lawmen and bankers. They may have been a candle in the wind, but while they lasted, they shed a lot of light.

The Poes were Texas folks, a very large family until cholera got both parents and two children. But our story starts a little later in Indian Territory, when Adolphus Lane Poe—called Pony—and his brother Bill rustled a herd of horses near Fort Supply. Pony got himself caught and went up the river for three years for that one, courtesy of the Honorable Isaac Parker, better known as the "hanging judge" of the US District Court for the Western District of Arkansas, all the law there was west of Fort Smith. Brother Bill evaded the law for a while but was caught a little later and got six years of his own.

Pony was a suspect in at least one crime after that, and when Bill got out of stir he soon indulged in a little armed robbery and went off for fifteen more years. But Pony stayed out of jail, married, raised a family, and lived on a hardscrabble farm near a place called Nuyaka. The family grew, and to his own kids was added Bill's son, Oscar, whose mother abandoned him on Pony's doorstep when Bill went back to prison.

Pony and Oscar turned out to be two of a kind, and Oscar had been picked up for horse theft by the time he was seventeen. This was a first offense—at least the first for anything this serious—and the law cut him some slack. A year later, in 1909, Oscar went to stealing horses again, again got caught, and this time got two years. Once he got out, he tried cattle rustling up in Oklahoma, and this time he got five years' hard time.

Paroled in 1915, he went to work in the Oklahoma oil patch until, a month or so into his new life, he tried to sell a company team and wagon to a rival oil company. The potential buyer smelled a large rat, but when two peace officers came to arrest Oscar, he opened fire on them, badly wounding both. What to do? Why back to the welcoming arms of Uncle Pony at his out-of-the-way ranch.

And here he was not only safe from the law, but chanced to meet the Hart brothers, Harrison and William, twin survivors of an impoverished family from Centralia, Oklahoma, a wide spot in the road up toward Vinita. It was a match made in heaven, for the Harts were on the run, too. They had been accused of burglary, among others things, and Will had complicated things by shooting the local schoolmaster, the ostensible reason being that the teacher had scolded his sister for some sort of classroom misbehavior.

And so the Harts came to meet Pony Poe, who hired them on to ride his blooded horses. Both young men had been jockeys, but in addition to riding for Pony, they spent some time in petty theft around Nuyaka. And it was probably then that Pony recruited them into his horse-stealing operation.

For Pony was into a very good thing. It was the winter of 1915-16, World War I was raging, and the European combatants were buying horses at a prodigious rate. Oscar and Will played large roles in the theft of other people's herds, which were then stashed in remote canyons until they could be marketed. Oscar and Will got themselves caught rustling, however, and spent some time in jail in Nowata County.

That time wasn't wasted, however, since the boys met a couple of kindred spirits, Russell Tucker and Jess Littrell. Littrell had been around; he had spent a couple of years in federal prison for—what else?—horse theft and afterward tried his hand at bootlegging. It got him arrested in 1911, 1912, and 1915. Tucker had joined him in the marketing of ardent spirits, bonded him out, and hit the road for the high lonesome. They were Pony's kind of kids.

Business was booming in the horse market, and Pony soon decided he needed more help. He found it in brothers Floyd, Lee, and Glenn Jarrett and brother-in-law Ab Connor. All of them had been pains in the neck to the local law for years. The Jarretts were a memorable piece of work. They came from a huge family, of which seven out of ten brothers turned bad. They were not master criminals, certainly, as one story relates.

Ab, Lee, and Glenn went off to rob a train in the spring of 1911, with the master moron of the criminal world, Elmer McCurdy. Elmer later won some small claim to fame by getting himself killed by the law but still carving out a stellar postmortem career: He spent many years touring raree shows as a dummy, permanently dead and ossified with arsenic. But he still enjoyed a time in the limelight he had never achieved in life, until he was finally discovered for what he really was when his arm fell off during a filming of *The Six Million Dollar Man*.

On this job, this band of boobies blew the express car safe to get at all that money; only, they used far too much nitroglycerin and blew the car apart and the safe out into a field. Curses! Foiled again!

Gang member Walter Jarrett robbed a bank in Prue, Oklahoma, fought the pursuing lawmen, and the law won. The rest of this fragrant little bunch went their nefarious ways. Glenn Jarrett was especially active; it got him five years in the Kansas State Prison. Oscar and Will Hart stuck together, and rustling on the grand scale proceeded apace. Pony Poe's army expanded to include not only Oscar and the Harts, but also other Hart brothers, Lee Jarrett, and Red Cloud Scruggs.

The gang graduated now to armed robbery, pulling several jobs in Coffeyville, Kansas, not so long before of the bloody end of the Dalton gang. After several forays to that long-suffering little town, they moved south into Oklahoma for a bit, then back to Coffeyville.

It was a typically stupid act. Oscar and Will had a pair of floozies with them, and the object of their trip was plainly not business but pleasure. But they were recognized and finally forced to surrender. The evidence they carried with them was overwhelming: cash—one of the women had almost twelve hundred dollars shoved into her corset—gold coins, a stolen pistol, and jewelry, including a wedding ring stolen right there in Coffeyville.

It got better. With Will and Oscar in jail, they began to have an interesting visitor, none other than Pony Poe, packing a handgun and a great wad of cash. He was a cattle buyer, he said, and in spite of several days' interrogation he remained a mystery, finally released for insufficient evidence.

And then, the night before Will and Oscar were to be shipped to Oklahoma for trial, several of the rest of the gang broke both men out, first getting the law to take one of their members inside masquerading as a drunk. He opened the door for the others, and all of them, including Will and Oscar, were gone.

A whole string of robberies followed down in Oklahoma. Meanwhile, Pony had arrived in Independence, Kansas, to bail out Mabel Brooks, apparently Oscar's common-law wife. Unfortunately for Pony, an alert official recognized some of the bail money bills as among those stolen in one of the gang's robberies. Pony was back in the slammer.

The next act was played out in Nowata, Oklahoma, where a carload of men robbed, of all things, a meat market, which they looted of divers supplies, including a whole hog carcass. A couple of carloads of citizens followed the bandits' car; its tracks led one group of them to Big Blue Canyon, a brushy, rocky, wilderness used as a refuge as far back as the Civil War, and allegedly even by the Dalton gang. It was crawling with rattlesnakes and riddled with caves, a very bad place to go man-hunting in.

There was a four-citizen posse, led by the town marshal, and the five walked up on the big automobile parked close to the canyon's mouth. They walked too far, for about the time they decided they ought to back away and get some reinforcements, the outlaws opened up on them.

The marshal was killed, and two of the citizens fell, too, one of them mortally wounded; the other was seriously hurt but would survive. Only two possemen stayed in action, and one of them thought he had hit one of their attackers with a shotgun round. The bandits chose to get on with their flight rather than try to finish off the little posse, and so they set fire to the possemen's car, climbed into their own automobile, and roared away.

This left the population of little Delaware, Oklahoma, to mourn two of their most popular citizens. Most everybody came to the funerals, a choir sang "sometime, we'll understand," and the dozens of lawmen who attended the marshal's funeral left with a new and bitter resolve.

Then the bandits showed the stupid streak so common to their kind. Tucker and Littrell whooped it up at a dance. They boasted to a couple of flirtatious ladies that they were big, bold bank robbers who intended to rob the bank at Okemah very shortly. The women passed this incautious bragging on to the law, which immediately heightened security.

It turned out that the target bank was in the town of Harrah, and the robbery was successful, netting some four thousand dollars' worth of goods, even down to the mean-spirited theft of a banker's diamond stickpin. Citizen posses pursued unsuccessfully, and the trail went cold—until, that is, a typical stupid bandit episode: Jess Littrell and Russell Tucker blandly returned to town by train. They went to the local home of one Joe Welsher, where a large posse surrounded them.

After negotiations and agreement to release Welsher's wife and children, the bandits instead surrounded themselves with the Welsher family and bolted out the back door, firing as they went. The posse held their fire to save the Welshers, and such few shots as they could get off were ineffective. One posseman commented later, "I believe in the future, I'll stick to my office job."

So the outlaws got away clean, escaping two brushes with other posses, stealing a car, and finally rousting out a cabdriver named Fuller, whom they paid to drive them to Boley, an all-black town east of Oklahoma City. There they stuck up a schoolteacher in a buggy, jammed a gun in his ribs, and forced him to drive them farther. When they finally let the schoolteacher go, the teacher drove "at a furious pace" to find some law. Once he did so, the long hunt was finally over.

The bandits had taken refuge in a local home, and once the posse arrived, they ran wildly out the back door, shooting as they ran and headed for the dubious safety of a chicken coop. Tucker didn't make it, drilled through the head by a posseman's bullet. Then the law made the mistake of summoning Littrell to surrender; the answer was a blast of fire that killed a deputy, whose last words were said to be "I wish I hadn't came here."

The posse responded with a torrent of fire, nearly tearing the chicken coop apart, and Littrell, hit repeatedly, changed his mind about surrender. He had been hit five times, including a round through one lung. The posse recovered more than one thousand dollars in loot and even the treasured stickpin.

Once Littrell had been moved to jail in Okemah, Sheriff Jones was faced with a new problem: A substantial portion of the citizenry was talking about a lynching party. The sheriff got his badly wounded charge out of town, and with a stop for emergency medical help, he got Littrell to the state prison at McAlister.

Now the hunt for the rest of the gang got some help, a tip on the gang's whereabouts. Among other helpful events, the hunters arrested a young felon who had escaped the Vinita jailhouse with Poe and Hart. This young man regurgitated a complex tissue of lies and excuses about the gang, including the tale that Oscar intended to set the all-time outlaw record by hitting *three* banks in the same town. Maybe so, but he would never get the chance.

The law's attention centered on the Nuyaka Mission country, a wild brushy area not far from—where else—Pony Poe's place. In a spot called Hell Hole Canyon, they found the bandits' empty camp, just a tent and the remains of a fire. On the thesis that the bandits might be back, the posse waited. They were right.

After a miserable wait in the snow through a bitter night, the posse saw their quarry returning to the campsite. Spotting the lawmen, the outlaws opened fire, and a wild fight followed. Oscar and Will Hart charged the posse, showering their position with Winchester rounds, but the law's aim was better. Oscar and Will were hit hard multiple times. Will fell motionless in the snow, but Oscar crawled for cover, now banging away with his pistol. Harry Hart took a bullet near the left eye, and he too went down to stay.

Oscar, still firing, was finally hit by a rifle bullet in the head, and that, as they say, "was all she wrote." Only one posse member had been hurt, and his wound was only superficial.

It had been a smashing victory for the law; the only fly in their ointment was the small amount of loot recovered. Stories of hidden loot were inevitable, but decades of searchers have come up empty in this wild area.

What was left of the outlaws was entrusted to the ministrations of the Okmulgee Furniture and Funeral Company. There was much excitement over the good guys' triumph. Even Oscar's widow, Mabel, showed up, to tell the press that she had tried and tried to turn Oscar from the paths of evil, but there was just no saving him. She also said—and this was far closer to the truth—that the Poe family was responsible for his vile deeds, "a pack of thieves who are beyond redemption."

Mabel seemed to have plenty of money; her baggage required three men to move it, and she paid for clothing and high-grade coffins for the burial of all three men. Facing charges of receiving stolen property and harboring fugitives up in Kansas, she sniffed, "a widow is not well treated in the state of Kansas."

She departed Oklahoma by train . . . but not to Kansas.

Jess Littrell finally recovered enough to be dealt with. He was moved to Oklahoma County to face charges there, and he got twenty-five years. He was then moved back to Okemah and given life for murder. He could look forward to another murder trial in Nowata County in the unlikely event that he lived long enough. Lee Jarrett was picked up off a road in 1921, right next to a wrecked Ford, stone dead, apparently as a result of some drunk driving with at least one other wanted criminal, who was nowhere to be seen.

Which left Pony Poe. Pony saw the handwriting on the wall after the Poe-Hart gang was no more. He not only moved to Texas but changed his name. Leaving his family, he wandered across the West, working, among other things, as bootlegger, oil-field worker, and laborer.

He did at least one more stretch in the pen out in New Mexico on a charge of larceny. While confined, he killed a man, but he had his first good luck in quite some time: A guard saw the killing and said it was self-defense.

Pony spent his last years sponging off his distant relatives, still drifting from job to job. He had lost the allegiance of his close family, once they found out he had long had a second "family" up in New Mexico. He did visit a daughter in the 1950s, a reunion that ended when Pony shot and killed his son-in-law after some sort of domestic dispute, later ruled justifiable homicide.

Pony died in a 1963 car wreck in Ardmore, Oklahoma. He was eighty-seven and crooked to the end. No driver's license, but three social security cards. He ended up in an indigent's grave.

CHAPTER 24

The Scourge of the Railroad

The Sontags

As John and George Sontag and their cohort Chris Evans told the story, they were just poor boys pushed around by that big bully of a railroad, and all they were really doing was getting even. In the last quarter of the nineteenth century, that glib explanation aroused a lot of sympathy from the people of California's San Joaquin Valley. The general distaste for the railroad was ignited by what were seen to be exorbitant freight rates and the seizure of much rich farmland for the railroad's right-of-way. Then there was the burning memory of the Mussel Slough fight, which pitted some twenty local men against a railroad party, which included a deputy US marshal. Seven men died, in what many saw as more aggression by a brutal railroad.

That anger was understandable. But it did not do much to justify the brothers' unrestricted violence, the dead men left in the brothers' wake . . . or the widows and orphans. Their private war on the Southern

Pacific was a good excuse for robbing trains, but it didn't show much concern for the railroad's ordinary employees, the men who were put at risk by the brothers' jihad.

The boys were born of good parents up in Mankato, Minnesota, not far from Northfield, scene of the earlier James-Younger gang disaster. They came of good stock; their father, Jacob Conant, a carpenter and a native of Holland, was killed in an accident early in their lives. Their mother remarried; her new husband was Mathias Sontag, a German-born entrepreneur who served in the Civil War. Afterward he opened first a dry-goods store and later a hotel and restaurant, the Mankato House, which was the first hotel in the city.

He and his wife had several more children. Growing up, the boys got a good, solid parochial education, for the whole family was Catholic, but temptation wasn't long in coming. George, the younger brother, got into trouble early, when at the age of fifteen he stole some cigars from his employer and spent some time in reform school up in Minnesota. A little later he did some more time in the pen in Omaha, Nebraska. Whatever lessons time in prison was supposed to teach didn't take.

Meanwhile brother John was working for ol' devil Southern Pacific out in California; he managed to get himself hurt on the job, and afterward he said the Southern Pacific had not given him the care he needed. Then, he said, the railroad wouldn't rehire him after he healed up. Just who did what to whom when, and why, remains lost in the mists of time, but John's fury with the railroad remained and only seemed even to increase with time as he brooded over it. Still angry, he went to work on a ranch owned by one Chris Evans, who was also an impassioned and vociferous critic of the railroad. They were made for each other.

The two men leased a livery stable in the valley town of Modesto, but in about a year a fire destroyed not only the structure but the horses as well. Whether they blamed the fire on Southern Pacific, too, they turned to crime as their next life's work.

They found hiding places up around Susanville, then a comparatively remote area, places called Roop's Fort or Fort Defiance. From these hideouts, they attacked the Southern Pacific, using the same simple, effective tactics. First they selected a suitable point to stage their robbery and stashed their horses there. Next they boarded the train; no tickets, of course, just a short period of hiding on the train from the inevitable railroad detectives.

The last act was also simple. At their predetermined point of attack, the brothers jumped out of their hiding place, shoved their guns into the engineer's face, and directed an unauthorized stop. Then came the dynamite, tearing open the express car safe, and Sontag and Evans were on their way with a sack of booty.

Once George was out of jail up in Minnesota, Chris and John joined him there. The three tried another train robbery and were successful, although they didn't get much loot. What they did get was the attention of the Pinkerton Agency, which contracted to oversee railroad security.

And they should have stayed in Minnesota, rather than returning to California. They tried another train, all three of them, but this holdup was a bust. All the cash there was, was some five hundred dollars; the rest of the loot was a heap of coin, too much to carry; worse still, the coins were Peruvian and Mexican, substantially worthless to the outlaws.

There was worse to come. In August 1892, the gang was in Visalia in the San Joaquin Valley, when the police finally found them. In a wild gun battle, George and Chris managed to shoot their way out, but John didn't make it. Chris and George ran for it, into the rugged Sierra Nevada, with an estimated three hundred civilian possemen and assorted bounty hunters searching for them, in addition to regular peace officers.

The result was chaos. One lawman estimated that a proliferation of friendly fire clashes left "at least 11 deputies . . . seriously wounded by other officers. Anyone who went deer hunting during this time was in danger of being shot by over-zealous posses."

But with so many pursuers in the field, inevitably the two outlaws ran into some of them. In September, in a wild eight-hour shootout that was later called the "battle of Sampson's Flat," an officer and a posseman died, and Chris Evans lost an eye to a round in the head. Badly hurt as Evans was, however, the pair still got away.

The hunt went on through the winter of 1892–93. Evans and Sontag evaded their pursuers. They had some help. So many people in the San Joaquin hated the Southern Pacific, that there were lots of chances for shelter and food and information. And there is a charming story about Evans's daughter Eva, who followed a posse tracking her father and Sontag and boldly fired a shot to warn them the law was on their tracks.

But then, in the summer of 1893, some new leadership took over for the law. Marshal George Gard was underwhelmed by the mass of man hunters falling all over each other in the valley. He changed strategies, opting for a very small, select posse that could move, hunt, and gather information without alerting the whole countryside. The new tactics paid off. The marshal at last got some solid intel that his quarry intended to stop at Evans's wife's home, at a place on the Patterson ranch near Visalia.

There is a tale, probably apocryphal, that the outlaws, realizing they had worn out their welcome in the San Joaquin Valley, decided to flee, allegedly to South Africa. Evans contacted his wife with directions to "wire Sontag's dad and ask for $100." Somehow, the law learned of this and that the outlaws were going to "sneak back to the Evans's Visalia home to pick up the dough. The sheriffs were waiting. . . ." Well, maybe.

The marshal and his men did not go blundering off to the Evans house, as some previous posses would have done. Instead, he set up shop nearby with three other men in an old cabin at a place called Stone Corral. Gard knew there was some measurable chance the outlaws might either come there or ride by, and so he and his posse remained out of sight and alert.

And at last he caught sight of the outlaws riding cautiously toward the cabin. The lawmen held their fire, but Evans saw one of them and opened fire; in the wild firefight that followed, Fred Jackson, a Nevada policeman, hit Evans with a shotgun round. The outlaws took cover, but the only shelter they could find was a haystack. It was pretty fair concealment, but it didn't do a thing to stop bullets or shot.

All through most of the night the fight went on. The outlaws couldn't run, and the officers dared not advance. One attempt by the marshal got him only a bad bullet wound in the knee. He sensibly called for reinforcements from Visalia and elected to wait for them and for daylight.

Sontag had been badly hit during the night, a round that tore through his belly. The pain was so bad that around dawn he pleaded with Evans to kill him. Evans refused, at which time Sontag told him to run for it and tried to shoot himself. He couldn't manage that, only stunning himself; when he came back to consciousness, the pain was worse than ever. He lay suffering on a pile of straw and manure through the rest of the night.

Evans at last ran into the gloom and disappeared. He was carrying wounds to his shoulder and belly but still managed to walk some six miles to a homesteader's cabin and asked the occupants to at least bandage his wounds. He took refuge there, but these homesteaders elected to send a message to the law. A large posse answered, prepared for a fight, but Evans had at last had enough and surrendered. Evans went off to jail in Visalia, the same jail where Sontag now lay dying. Evans had one arm amputated, and Sontag passed away on the third of July.

The story goes that after George Sontag learned of his brother's death, he and four other convicts attempted to escape from Folsom. The escape was a disaster: Sontag and another con were wounded, and the other three were killed.

George did another fifteen years up the river, until he was pardoned by President Teddy Roosevelt in 1908. Like Cole Younger, he went on the road with a lecture all about "crime does not pay," appearing in the Opera House at Mankato, his hometown, where he was "well received." And in 1915 he produced a film, predictably called *The Folly of a Life of Crime* and starring himself. He topped that off with a ghostwritten book called *A Pardoned Lifer*. Who says crime doesn't pay?

Which left the indestructible Evans. In 1893 he got a life sentence in Folsom, but before he could be shipped there, he escaped and stayed on the loose for a month and a half. Then it was back to prison until the spring of 1911. He was paroled—one of the conditions of parole being "banishment" from California—and went off to homestead in Oregon. He died in 1917.

CHAPTER 25

A Rich Assortment of Trash

Some Lesser Scum

Not all of the criminal family acts produced deathless prose, memorable crime waves, or spectacular tales of robberies, escapes, and derring-do. Many were simply sordid stories of casual murder and brutality by people who became convinced that they were somehow too good to work like other folks. Flouting the law, brutalizing others, and putting them down somehow made these misfits somebody special in their own eyes, however insignificant they really were as human beings.

This book has dealt with some of the more famous—or infamous—of the criminal blood relations, the well-known names and their storied crimes. Here are a few of the others, especially sorry specimens with no claim to memory except family connection . . . and pure evil.

THE ESPINOSAS

There are two distinctly different versions of the Espinosa epic. The first is this:

There were three of them, Julian, Victorio, and Felipe, Mexican citizens who came north across the border about 1861 with the avowed aim of killing "100 gringos." They said they had revenge in mind, a noble retribution for six relatives "killed in the Mexican War." They would begin their campaign of vengeance in Colorado, where they busily set about murdering people they didn't know.

Some of the gloss rubbed off their noble motives when they not only killed but also robbed some of their victims, and that after the victims had been recently paid. There were twenty-six killings in two years, until Felipe, the terrorist leader, gave the lie to the brothers' noble motives by offering to stop the war if he received a land grant of some five thousand acres. The state responded to this nonsensical proposition by posting a reward for Felipe, dead or alive.

Various vigilante groups joined in the hunt, but they seem to have caught and lynched only sundry non-Espinosas. Until, that is, Victorio was at last run down out in Fairplay, California, and attached to a tree, whereof he expired.

Along the way, the army had gotten into the hunt and at last intelligently hired Tom Tobin, a scout with a considerable reputation. He would live up to it.

Operating all alone, Tobin ran down the two remaining Espinosas and shot both quite dead, presumably without trying overhard to get them to surrender. Since Tobin had an understandable interest in the reward, he carefully removed his quarry's heads as proof positive of their demise and took them back with him to Fort Garland.

Given the reputation of the dead men, they, or rather their heads, became a popular attraction for the curious. When the rest of the brothers were long gone, the heads remained in circulation, last seen exhibited at sideshows by one Kit Carson III. Carson turned out to be none other than Tobin's grandson, and when at last so-called "experts" solemnly pronounced the heads to be phony, Carson announced that "he had always said" the real Espinosa heads were buried back at Fort Garland.

Version number two, a little more complicated, goes like this: The brothers Espinosa were but two, Jose and Vivian, from a family resident in New Mexico; they thought either that the hated Anglos had wrongfully taken part of their land, or that an Espinosa child had been killed and their sheep run off. Once they started their vendetta with the "Anglos," they sent a letter to the governor offering to call off their feud if the state paid appropriate compensation for the wrongly seized family land.

Their first enormity was robbing a wagon belonging to a priest, tying the driver to the wagon tongue, then whipping up the wagon team. It is not recorded whether they even knew the driver. Fortunately, the priest was nearby and got the team stopped while the driver was still mostly in one piece, but the Espinosas were only beginning.

Over the next weeks, the brothers continued their killing spree, murdering people they didn't even know. After murdering William Bruce at his sawmill on Hardscrabble Creek, they killed "Uncle" Henry Harkens, a well-known and much-respected sawmill owner. Him they shot, before chopping his head into several chunks with an ax.

Next came five more settlers in the South Park area, and by this time ad hoc vigilance committees were organized, one of which arrested and hanged a man named Baxter . . . only he was the wrong one. It was a little late to apologize when the violence continued after Baxter's death.

At last the Espinosa boys were identified as the culprits when they shot a man named Metcalf, peacefully hauling a wagonload of lumber. Metcalf's terrified team promptly galloped off, taking their owner to safety. He had nothing worse then a bruised chest, for the Espinosa bullet had hit a thick wad of paper in Metcalf's breast pocket.

That prompted a search of every inch of South Park, a dogged hunt that at last turned up the Espinosa boys, who were bombarded with shotgun rounds until Jose was killed very dead. His brother managed to escape in the excitement, "mistaken for a member of the posse," however unlikely that sounds.

Vivian, lacking everything but venom, found a replacement for his brother; his choice tells you a lot about Vivian's character, for his recruit was his nephew, all of twelve years old. The two stopped a wagon carrying an Anglo man and his Mexican wife. The man escaped, running up a mountainside with the killers chasing him; the woman hid behind a boulder until another wagon appeared, driven by Pedro Garcia.

Garcia told her to hide in the wagon, and when the Espinosas returned from their futile pursuit of the husband, Garcia stoutly denied he had seen her. Yes, he said, he had seen a gringo man running away a while ago, but not a lady. About that time the lady raised her head, however, and the Espinosas ordered Garcia to "put that prostitute of the American out of the wagon or we will open fire."

The lady nobly cried out, "Don Pedro, don't die for me; they are Christians, and won't hurt me," or something like that. Helpless, Garcia drove off, and the "Christian" Vivian tied up the woman and raped her.

Soldiers from Fort Garland took up the search for the Espinosas, and they found the kidnapped woman, shaken and brutalized but alive. And then they brought in the first team, expert scout Tom Tobin, who lived with his Mexican wife and daughter just across the New Mexico line.

Tobin was, as the lawyers say, sui generis, one of a kind. He sounds a little like television's Paladin, habitually wearing black clothing and riding a black horse. He was a two-gun man, too, but for all that a good citizen, president of his local school board even though he was illiterate himself.

Tobin was offered a reward of at least fifteen hundred dollars to bring in the Espinosas, a good deal of money in 1863. And so, followed by two soldiers and a Mexican boy, he tracked the outlaws until he saw crows circling far ahead. He guessed, it turned out correctly, that the Espinosas were busy butchering an ox they had stolen.

Maybe that's why the Espinosas didn't see Tobin until he was very close to his quarry, so close that when Vivian grabbed for his gun, Tobin put a bullet in him from his muzzle-loading rifle. "Jesus favor me!" Vivian is said to have cried—or something like that—and yelled to his nephew to run for it. "Escape! I am killed!"

The soldiers shot at the fleeing youngster and missed, but Tobin, quickly reloading, did not. He broke the nephew's back with a single round, killing him.

There remained dealing finally with Vivian Espinosa, who still had some life left in him, enough to reach his pistol and shoot at one of the soldiers. He missed, and Tobin stepped in to disarm Vivian, flop him down across a log, and summarily amputate his head. The Mexican boy with Tobin was sent to remove the nephew's head as well, and Tobin delivered both trophies to the command at Fort Garland in a gunnysack, proof positive of a mission accomplished.

Besides the heads, Tobin and his party brought back a sort of diary kept by the Espinosas. They had killed twenty-two Anglos, it read, and maybe that was so. In any case, Tobin had done Colorado a great favor.

It took Tom Tobin a long time to get his reward—nothing has changed with the federal government—but he was presented with a beautiful silver-mounted knife and two hundred dollars by a private citizen. There was a story that the reward had been advertised at twenty-five hundred dollars, but no evidence of that has survived.

Either version of the end of the Espinosa menace is about equally satisfying. The motives of the Espinosas will always remain unclear, but if there was anything remotely noble about them, the rape of a helpless woman should have put that myth to rest.

THE MANLEYS

The Manley boys, Amos and Abler, don't get much space here, but then, they don't deserve much, being the worst kind of trash, not only killers but rank ingrates as well.

They rode into history back in 1880, when they sought the hospitality of a small farmer down along the border between the Choctaw and Creek nations. Now a place to sleep and maybe a meal were common favors most people did for travelers in those simpler times, when hospitality to strangers was a common virtue even with people without much in the way of money or other resources. So it was with the Ellis McVay family in December of that far-off year.

On a bitter night Amos and Abler stopped after dark at the little McVay cabin, occupied by Ellis, Mrs. McVay, their two children, and their hired hand, William Burnett. "We're on our way to find work over in the Choctaw nation," they said, "and would sure appreciate some shelter on this bitter night."

The McVay family made room in their tiny abode, and the visitors settled in on a pallet in a corner. The McVays' hospitality was repaid in the dead of night, when the Manleys crept over to McVay and Amos shot him in the head. Abler shot the farmer twice in the gut. Burnett, the hired hand, got to his own gun and stepped up to defend Mrs. McVay and the children. He occupied the ruffians long enough that Mrs. McVay and the kids got away, running barefoot into the bitter night.

The gutsy Burnett went down with a slash across his neck and his right hand entirely cut off. The Manleys assumed he was dead—he wasn't—and left, mercifully without following Mrs. McVay and her children into the darkness.

The killers' flight didn't do them any good. They were run down and captured the following day and shipped off to the fabled US District Court at Fort Smith, where "Hanging Judge" Isaac Parker presided. Now Parker was a good judge and a fair man despite his fearsome nickname; he would hang fewer than one hundred of the scum of the earth during his many years on the bench, but since he tried more than ten thousand felonies, the percentage of death sentences was in fact quite low.

But there would be no mercy for the murderous Manleys. Among the other pieces of evidence introduced at their trial was the gallant Burnett's severed hand; the jury convicted and the Manleys went to the Fort Smith gallows in September of 1881.

Good riddance.

EPILOGUE

These tales of extinct criminals are just a sample of the myriad of stories about bad-acting kin. There are lots more out there, equally vile, at least enough of them for a second volume. They all came from a clannish era, a time when kin stuck together and were most reluctant to talk to the "laws," as people in the South and Southwest sometimes called policemen and sheriff's deputies.

What is most amazing to folks today were the lengths to which relatives would go to protect men obviously guilty of major felonies, including murder. That sort of thing still happens today, of course, but our perception is that it is at least less common.

Maybe that's a function of the so-called "mellowing" of society, although that seems most unlikely in view of the often bizarre nature of today's crimes. Older days didn't see as much of people murdering other people because mysterious voices told them to, or because Allah willed it, or because they were upset with an exacting boss, or because people at work were mean to them, or because somebody "looked at them hard," the alleged justification for a recent murder.

There was some of that, to be sure, but most of the truly nasty felonious behavior was strictly business. A few of the horse outlaws and automobile bandits enjoyed killing, especially killing lawmen—Larry DeVol is a good example of that sort of scum—but mostly the outlaw life was attractive because it seemed to be a road to riches without much work.

A lot of the bleeding was done by merchants and travelers and bank tellers, even innocent bystanders, and there were lots of widows and orphaned kids. But most of the casualties belonged to overworked, underpaid lawmen.

Here's to their memory.

BIBLIOGRAPHY

Baker, Pearl. *The Wild Bunch at Robber's Roost*. Lincoln, NE: Bison Books, 1989.

Block, Eugene B. *Great Train Robberies*. London: Alvin Redman, 1964.

Butler, Ken. *More Oklahoma Renegades*. Gretna, LA: Pelican Publishing, 2007.

Cain, Del. *Lawmen of the Old West: The Bad Guys*. Plano: Republic of Texas Press, 2001.

Cook, D. J. *Hands Up*. Norman: University of Oklahoma Press, 1958.

Cunningham, Eugene. *Triggernometry*. Caldwell, ID: Caxton Printers, 1989.

Dalton, Emmett. *Beyond the Law*. Coffeyville, KS: Coffeyville Historical Society, 2005.

Dary, David. *True Tales of Old-Time Kansas*. Lawrence: University Press of Kansas, 1984.

DeArment, Robert. *Bravo of the Brazos*. Norman: University of Oklahoma Press, 2002.

———. *Deadly Dozen: Forgotten Gunfighters of the Old West*. Vol. 2. Norman: University of Oklahoma Press, 2007.

———. *Deadly Dozen: Twelve Forgotten Gunfighters of the Old West.* Vol. 1. Norman: University of Oklahoma Press, 2003.

Drago, Harry Sinclair. *Road Agents and Train Robbers: Half a Century of Western Banditry.* New York: Dodd, Mead & Co., 1973.

Edge, L. L. *Run The Cat Roads.* New York: Dembner Books, 1981.

Elman, Robert. *Badmen of the West.* Secaucus, NJ: Ridge Press, 1974.

Erdoes, Richard. *Saloons of the Old West.* New York: Gramercy Press, 1997.

Ernst, Robert R. *Robbin' Banks and Killin' Cops.* Baltimore: PublishAmerica, 2009.

Fisher, O. C., and J. C. Dykes. *King Fisher, His Life and Times.* Norman: University of Oklahoma Press, 1966.

Fulton, Maurice G. *History of the Lincoln County War.* Tucson: University of Arizona Press, 2008.

Garrett, Pat F. *The Authentic Life of Billy the Kid.* New York: Indian Head Books, 1994.

Geary, Rick. *The Saga of the Bloody Benders.* New York: Nantier, Beall, Minoustchine, 2007.

Girardin, G. Russell, and William J. Helmer. *Dillinger, The Untold Story.* Bloomington: Indiana University Press, 2008.

Hamilton, Stanley. *Machine Gun Kelly's Last Stand.* Lawrence: University Press of Kansas, 2003.

Hardy, Allison. *Kate Bender, The Kansas Murderess: The Horrible History of an Arch Killer.* Girard, KS: Haldeman-Julius Publications, 1944.

Helmer, William J., and Rick Mattix. *The Complete Public Enemy Almanac.* Nashville, TN: Cumberland House, 2007.

Horan, James D. *Desperate Men.* New York: Corgi Books, 1956.

James, John T. *The Benders in Kansas.* Pittsburg, KS: Mostly Books, 1995.

Jennings, Alphonso. *Beating Back.* Charleston, SC: Bibliobazaar, 2009.

Jessen, Ken. *Colorado Gunsmoke.* Loveland, CO: J. V. Publications, 1986.

Kelly, Charles. *The Outlaw Trail.* Old Saybrook, CT: Konecky and Konecky, 1999.

King, Jeffery S. *The Life and Death of Pretty Boy Floyd.* Kent, OH: Kent State University Press, 2008.

Koblas, John J. *Robbers of the Rails.* St. Cloud, MN: North Star Press, 2003.

Koch, Michael. *The Kimes Gang.* Bloomington, IN: AuthorHouse, 2005.

Maxwell, Hu. *Evans and Sontag.* Fresno, CA: Pioneer Publishers, 1981.

McPherson, M. A., and Eli McLaren. *Outlaws and Lawmen of the Old West.* Vol 1. Renton, WA: Lone Pine Publishing, 2000.

Metz, Leon Claire. *John Selman, Gunfighter.* Norman: University of Oklahoma Press, 1966.

———. *Pat Garrett.* Norman: University of Oklahoma Press, 1974.

———. *The Shooters.* El Paso, TX: Mangan Books, 1976.

Miller, Nyle H., and Joseph W. Snell. *Great Gunfighters of the Kansas Cowtowns.* Lincoln: University of Nebraska Press, 1967.

Morgan, R. D. *Bad Boys of the Cookson Hills.* Stillwater, OK: New Forums Press, 2002.

———. *Bandit Kings of the Cookson Hills.* Stillwater, OK: New Forums Press, 2003.

———. *The Tri-State Terror: The Life and Crimes of Wilbur Underhill.* Stillwater, OK: New Forums Press, 2005.

Myers, John M. *The Tombstone Story.* New York: Grosset and Dunlap, 1950.

Nash, Jay Robert. *Encyclopedia of Western Lawmen and Outlaws.* New York: DaCapo Press, 1994.

———. *Hustlers and Con Men.* New York: M. Evans & Co., 1976.

Neal, Bill. *Getting Away with Murder on the Texas Frontier*. Lubbock: Texas Tech University Press, 2006.

Newton, Willis, and Joe Newton. *The Newton Boys: Portrait of an Outlaw Gang*. Austin, TX: State House Press, 1994.

Nolan, Frederick. *The Lincoln County War*. Norman: University of Oklahoma Press, 1992.

O'Neal, Bill. *Encyclopedia of Western Gunfighters*. Norman: University of Oklahoma Press, 1979.

———. *Henry Brown, the Outlaw-Marshal*. College Station, TX: Creative Publishing Co., 1980.

Parsons, Chuck, and Marianne E. Hall Little. *Captain L. H. McNelly, Texas Ranger*. Austin, TX: State House Press, 2001.

Rasch, Phillip J. *Warriors of Lincoln County*. Stillwater, OK: NOLA, 1998.

Shirley, Glenn. *Red Yesterdays*. Wichita Falls, TX: Nortex Press, 1997.

———. *West of Hell's Fringe*. Norman: University of Oklahoma Press, 1978.

Skovlin, Jon M., and Donna McDaniel Skovlin. *In Pursuit of the McCartys*. Cove, OR: Reflections Publishing Co., 2001.

Smith, Robert Barr. *Daltons!* Norman: University of Oklahoma Press, 1996.

———. *Last Hurrah of the James-Younger Gang*. Norman: University of Oklahoma Press, 2001.

———. *Outlaw Tales of Oklahoma*. Guilford, CT: Globe Pequot Press, 2008.

———. *Tough Towns*. Guilford, CT: Globe Pequot Press, 2007.

Sonnichsen, C. L. *I'll Die Before I'll Run*. Lincoln: University of Nebraska Press, 1988.

———. *Pass of the North*. El Paso: Texas Western Press, 1968.

Swierczynski, Duane. *This Here's A Stick-Up*. Indianapolis, IN: Alpha, 2002.

Traywick, Ben. *Legendary Characters of Southeast Arizona.* Tombstone, AZ: Red Marie's Bookstore, 1994.

Warner, Opie. *A Pardoned Lifer; life of George Sontag.* San Bernardino, CA: Making of Modern Law Reprint from Harvard Law School Library.

Wilson, Colin. *World Famous Crimes.* New York: Carroll and Graf, 1995.

Wilson, R. Michael. *Encyclopedia of Stagecoach Robbery in Arizona.* Las Vegas, NV: RaMA Press, 2003.

Winters, Robert. *Mean Men: The Sons of Ma Barker.* Danbury, CT: Rutledge Books, 2000.

Wood, Fern Morrow. *The Benders: Keepers of the Devil's Inn.* Chelsea, MI: BookCrafters, 1992.

Yadon, Laurence J., and Dan Anderson. *Arizona Gunfighters.* Gretna, LA: Pelican Publishing, 2010.

Yadon, Laurence J., and Robert Barr Smith. *Old West Swindlers.* Gretna, LA: Pelican Publishing, 2011.

———. *Outlaws with Badges.* Gretna, LA: Pelican Publishing, 2012.

Index

A

Abshier, George, 12, 15
Alderman, Lloyd, 13, 14
Alvord, Burt, 43
Anderson, Hugh, 177–81
Anderson, Tom. *See* Christian, Bob
Anderson, William "Bloody Bill," 21
Anti-Horse Thief Association, 37, 133, 136

B

Bailey, Harvey, 88
Bailey, William, 176
Ball, Charlie, 4–6
Barker, Arthur "Doc," 86–87, 90–91, 92
Barker, Fred "Shorty," 86, 87–88, 89–91, 92, 94
Barker, George, 86, 87
Barker, Herman "Slim," 86, 87
Barker, Lloyd William "Red," 86, 89
Barker, "Ma," 14, 85–86, 87–89, 94
Barker gang and friends, 85–94
Barker-Inman-Terrill gang, 87
Barker-Karpis gang, 93–94
Barnes, Doug, 37
Beating Back (film), 164
Beating Back (Jennings), 156, 164
Behan, John, 123, 125
Bell, C. S., 111

Bender, John "Pa," 141–51
Bender, John (son), 141–51
Bender, Kate, 141–51
Bender, "Ma," 141–51
Benders: Keepers of the Devil's Inn (Wood), 151
Bennett, Warren, 136–37
Blackley, A. T., 63, 64, 65, 70
Bloody Mama (film), 89
bootleggers, 36–37
Boyle, John, 145
Breakenridge, Billy, 44, 49
Bremer, Edward, 86–87, 92
Broadwell, Dick, 2, 4, 6, 9
Brocius, Bill, 123
Brock brothers, 183–84
Brooks, Mabel, 198
Brooks, Willis, 162
Brown, HooDoo, 169
Brown, Joe, 84
Brown, Rube, 114
Bruce, William, 211
Burnett, William, 214, 215
Burrow, Jim, 183–84
Burrow, Rueben "Rube," 182–86
Bussey, Hess, 160

C

Cantelou, Jennie, 38
Carr, W. H. "Bill," 40
Casey, Dave, 116
Casey, Jim, 38, 116, 118–20
Casey, Vic, 38–39, 40, 116, 118–19

Cassidy, Butch, 60, 61
Cherryvale, KS, 144, 146
Christian, Bill, 35–49, 50, 119
Christian, Bob, 35–46, 49, 119
Clanton, Billy, 123, 126–27
Clanton, Isaac (Ike), 123–26, 128–29
Clanton, N. H. "Old Man," 123, 124
Clanton, Phinias "Phin," 123, 128
Clanton clan, 121–29
Clark, Arizona Donnie. *See* Barker, "Ma"
Clark, Ben, 49
Clements, Emmanuel "Mannen" (father), 78–80
Clements, Emmanuel "Mannie" (son), 78, 80, 84
Clements family, 78–84
Clifton, Dan "Dynamite Dick," 156, 159–60
Clum, John, 125
Coe, Phil, 103
Coffeyville, KS, 1–2, 197
Conant, Jacob, 204
Condon Bank, Coffeyville, KS, 1, 4–6
Connor, Ab, 196
Cox, Jim, 112
Cravatt, Gus, 132, 138
Cross, John, 134–35, 137
Crosswight, John, 117
Crotty, Billy, 146
Cuero Protection Club, 114

D
Dalton, Adeline, 3, 9
Dalton, Bill, 3, 9
Dalton, Bob, 2, 3–4, 6–7, 9
Dalton, Emmett, 2, 3, 4, 6–9, 10
Dalton, Gratton, 2–3, 4–6, 9
Dalton, Lewis, 3
Dalton brothers and gang, 1–10, 36
DeAutremont, Hugh, 51, 53–57, 58
DeAutremont, Ray, 51, 52–59
DeAutremont, Roy, 51, 53–58
Delta, CO, 59–73
DeMary, Major, 166
Desperate Men (Horan), 65
DeVol, Larry, 85, 90, 91, 93–94, 187
do-it-yourself-hanging-machine, 15
Doolin, Bill, 9–10, 36, 163
Dunlap, Three-Fingered Jack, 42–46, 49

E
Earp, Morgan, 128
Earp, Virgil, 125–26, 128
Earp, Warren, 128
Earp, Wyatt, 96, 121–22, 126, 128
Espinosa, Felipe, 210
Espinosa, Jose, 211–12
Espinosa, Victorio, 210
Espinosa, Vivian, 211–13
Evans, Chris, 203, 204–7, 208
Evans, Eva, 206
Everest, Wesley, 52

F

Farmer, Bert, 49
Farmer's and Merchant's Bank,
Delta, CO, 59, 60, 62–63
Farris, Sam, 38, 118
Ferguson, "Ma," 27
Fessenden, John, 40–41
Finlay, Jessie, 38, 40, 119
First National Bank, 1, 4, 6, 7, 11,
12, 61
Fisher, John "King," 104, 106
Fleagle, Jacob Henry "Little Jake,"
11–18
Fleagle, Jacob "Old Jake," 14–15
Fleagle, Ralph, 11–12, 15
Fly, Camillus, 43, 44, 128
Folly of a Life of Crime, The
(film), 208
Ford, Bob, 24
Foster, Joe, 106
Foy, Eddie, 104

G

Garcia, Pedro, 212
Gard, George, 206–7
Garrett, Billy, 178
Garrett, Pat, 82
Garver, J. H., 38–39, 40, 119
Giraud, Adolph, 167
Glasscock, Brent, 191–92
Great Northfield Minnesota Raid
(film), 19
Guadalupe Canyon, Mexico, 123

H

Haines, Wiley, 136–39

Hamm, William, 86–87, 92
Hardin, John Wesley, 78–79,
80–82, 95, 100, 113–14
Harkens, Henry, 211
Harmon, Jake, 117
Harris, Jack, 106
Hart, Harrison, 195–96, 197, 200
Hart, William, 195–96, 197, 200
Hassels, Sam, 42
Hayes, Bob, 42–46
Hays, Mary Ann, 63–64
Heinrich, Edward, 56
Helm, Jack "Captain," 110–11,
112, 113
Hereford, Red, 160
Herrera, Frank, 43
Hickok, Wild Bill, 103
Higgins, Fred, 46, 48
Hocker, W. E., 41
Holbrook, Foster, 41
Holliday, Doc, 96, 121, 125, 126
Hoover, J. Edgar, 85, 86, 88, 92
Horan, James D., 65, 66
Houston, Sam, 154
Houston, Temple, 154–56,
163, 164
Hull family, 130–31
Hurricane Minnie, 96

I

I'll Die Before I'll Run
(Sonnichsen), 113
Independent Order of Odd
Fellows (IOOF), 135
Indian Territory, 36–37, 107, 194

International Workers of the
    World (IWW), 52

J
Jackson, Fred, 207
James, Frank, 12, 22, 23, 24
James, Jesse, 19–20, 22, 24, 61, 164
James-Younger Gang, 19–25
Jarrett, Floyd, 196–97
Jarrett, Glenn, 196–97
Jarrett, Lee, 196–97, 201
Jarrett, Walter, 197
Jennings, Alphonso J. "Al," 36, 38,
    152–59, 161–64
Jennings, Ed, 154–56
Jennings, Frank, 152, 156, 158,
    161, 162, 163
Jennings, J. D. F., 38
Jennings, John, 154–58, 164
*Jesse James Meets Frankenstein's
    Daughter* (film), 19
Johnson, Crook-neck, 48
Johnson, Julia, 10
Johnson, Virgil, 30
Jones, Milt, 39, 41

K
Karpis, Alvin "Old Creepy," 85, 86,
    88, 89–93
Kearnes, Henry, 178
Kelly, Charles, 68
Kesinger, Everett, 12–13
Ketchum, Black Jack, 41, 49, 50
King, Frank, 43
Kloehr, John, 6, 7
Krum, Ed, 175

L
Larn, John, 95, 96–97
Lawson, George, 160
Laycock, Ben, 69–70
Laycock, Henry, 70
Leatherwood, Bob, 43, 44
Ledbetter, Bud, 157, 161, 162
Leslie, Frank, 123
Littleton, Captain, 110
Littrell, Jess, 196, 198–200, 201
Lonchar, George, 146
Loomis, Horace, 45–46
Lundgren, E. A., 12–13

M
Mackey, John, 37
Madsen, Chris, 118–19
Majors, Henry, 136, 137
Manley, Abler, 214–15
Manley, Amos, 214–15
Manson, Charles, 93
Martin, Sam, 130–39
Martin, Will, 130–39
Masterson, Bat, 96, 107, 173
Masterson, Ed, 173
Masterson, Jim, 173
Mather, Dave, 95, 169
McCarty, Bill, 60, 61, 62–66,
    68–70
McCarty, Fred, 60, 61, 62–67,
    68–70
McCarty, Tom, 60, 61, 62–66,
    68–69, 71–73
McCarty clan, 59–73
McCluskie, Arthur, 180–81
McCluskie, Mike, 175–79

McCluskie brothers, 173–81
McCurdy, Elmer, 152, 196
McKidrict, Joe, 99
McLowery, Tom, 123, 126–27
McNelly, Captain, 114
McVay, Ellis and family, 214
Medicine Lodge, KS, 179–80
Meik, Almira. *See* Bender, "Ma"
Miller, Clel, 23
Miller, Jim "Deacon Jim," 80, 82–83, 95, 96
Miller, Louis, 40–41
Milton, Jeff, 42, 45, 48, 49
Missouri Bushwhacker gangs, 21
Moffat, David, 61
Moran, Joe, 92
Morco, Happy Jack, 104
Morose, Beulah, 100
Morose, Martin, 100, 101
Morrison, Andy, 37
Musgrave, George, 42–46, 49

N
Newton, Dock, 188–92, 193
Newton, Jess, 188–92
Newton, Joe, 188–93
Newton, KS, 173–79
Newton, Willis, 187, 188–92, 193
Noe, Mark, 28
Nogales, AZ, 42–43
Northfield, MN, 19, 21–25, 63
Nutter, Lee, 159

O
O. Henry. *See* Porter, William Sydney

Oliver, Tony, 30
O'Malley, Morris, 156, 161, 162, 163
O'Malley, Pat, 156, 162, 163
Osage Indians, 136, 137
Outlaw, Bass, 99

P
Pardoned Lifer, A (Sontag), 208
Parker, Isaac "hanging judge," 21, 194, 214–15
Parker, Leroy. *See* Cassidy, Butch
Parrish, Amos, 12, 15
Parrish, John "Jaddo," 12, 15
Paxton, Charlie, 48
Pickering, William, 146
Pinkerton, William, 77
Pinkerton Agency, 75–77, 184, 205
Pitts, Charlie, 23, 24
Poe, Adolphus Lane "Pony," 194–96, 197–98, 201–2
Poe, Bill, 194–95
Poe, Mabel, 201
Poe, Oscar, 195, 196, 197, 198, 200
Poe-Hart gang, 194–202
Ponzilione, Father Paul, 146
Porter, William Sydney, 158
Pottawatomie County, OK, 36
Powers, Bill, 2, 4, 6, 9
Pruiett, Moman, 82

Q
Quantrill, William, 21, 172

R

Reeves, John, 41
Reno, Bill, 74–76, 77
Reno, Frank, 74–76, 77
Reno, John, 74–76
Reno, Simeon, 74–76, 77
Reynolds, Jim, 165, 168–71
Reynolds, John, 165, 168–72
Riley, Jim, 178, 179
Ringo, John, 80, 123, 128
Robinson, W. R., 63
Robson, Frank, 44
Royston, Howard, 12, 13–14, 15
Rudabaugh, Dave, 95, 169

S

San Miguel Bank, Telluride,
    CO, 61
Sanders, Red, 48
Scarborough, George, 101
Scott, Henry, 38
Scruggs, Cloud, 197
Seaman, Carey, 7
Selman, John, 78, 81, 95–101
Selman, John, Jr., 99, 100, 101
Selman, Thomas "Tom Cat," 95,
    96, 97
Simmons, Richard, 133–37
Simpson, Ray, 63–68, 69, 71–72
Singleterry, Owen, 169, 170, 171
Skeleton Canyon, AZ, 44
Slaughter, Gabe, 114
Slaughter, John, 44
Smith, George, 62
Sonnichsen, C. L., 113
Sontag, George, 203–4, 205–8

Sontag, John, 203–5
Sontag, Mathias, 204
Sowers, Joe, 146
Stiles, Bill, 23
Sutton, Bill, 112, 113, 114
Sutton, Willie, 188
Sutton-Taylor feud, 80, 109–15
Sylva, Nate, 117, 118

T

Taylor, Buck, 112
Taylor, Charley, 112
Taylor, Creed, 110
Taylor, Doboy, 110, 111–12
Taylor, Hays, 110, 111
Taylor, Jim, 113, 114, 115
Taylor, Josiah, 110
Taylor, Pink, 84
Taylor, Pitkin, 110, 113
Taylor, Rufus, 110
Taylor, Scrape, 114
Taylor, William "Bill," 110, 112,
    113, 115
Terrill, Ray, 85
Territorial Treasury, Denver,
    CO, 170
Texas Bankers Association, 190
Texas State Police, 112, 113
Third Northwestern National
    Bank of Minneapolis, 90
Thomas, Heck, 162–63
Thompson, Ben, 102–6, 107, 108
Thompson, Billy, 102, 103, 104,
    106–8
Tilghman, Bill, 163
Tin Hat Brigade, 97

Tobin, Tom, 210, 212–13
Tolbert, Paden, 157, 161, 162
Tombstone, AZ, 123, 124, 125
Tombstone (film), 121, 124
Townsend, Joe, 80
Travis, John, 67
Trew, John, 63
Trousdale, W. B. "Billy," 37
Tucker, Russell, 196, 198–99
Tumlinson, Old Joe, 112
Turner, Will, 37
Tuttle, Perry, 175, 177–78

V
Vaudeville Theater and Gambling
    Saloon, San Antonio, TX,
    104–6, 107

W
Ware, Dave, 134
Warner, Matt, 61, 62–63, 65
Welsher, Joe, 199
West, Little Dick, 156, 159, 160,
    162–63
Western Movement, 140–42
Wewoka Trading Company, 40
Wheeler, Richard, 181
White, Carpenter Gus, 39
Whitney, E. B., 104, 107
Wild Bunch at Robber's Roost, The
    (Kelly), 67–68
Wilde, Harry, 17
Williams, Ed. *See* Christian, Bill

Williams, Jesse. *See* Musgrave,
    George
Wilson, Ed, 41–42
Winters, Shelley, 89
Wolbert, H. H., 63, 64, 65, 70
Wood, Fern Morrow, 151
Wyatt, Zip, 36
Wyatt Earp (film), 121

Y
York, Alexander, 147, 150
York, Ed, 147
York, William, 146–48
Young, Code, 42–46
Young, Felix, 117
Young, Florence, 27
Young, James "J. D.", 26, 27
Young, Jennings, 26–27, 28–32, 33
Young, Lorena, 28–29, 31, 33
Young, Lyman Harry "Harry," 26,
    28–32, 33
Young, Oscar, 27, 29, 33
Young, Paul, 26–27
Young, Vinita, 28–29, 31, 33
Young, Willie Florence, 26, 27, 28,
    29, 31, 33, 34
*Young Men of America, A Sparkling
    Journal for Young Gentlemen*
    (magazine), 24–25
Younger, Cole, 22, 24, 61
Younger, John, 21
Younger, Thomas Coleman, 21
Younger brothers and gangs, 2, 18,
    19, 21, 22, 23–25, 61

About the Author

Robert Barr Smith entered the US Army as a private in 1958. He served in Vietnam with the 4th Infantry Division, a total of more than seven years in Germany, and with troop units and on posts throughout the United States, retiring as a colonel. He is a Senior Parachutist and holds the Legion of Merit (two awards), the Bronze Star, and other decorations.

He holds two degrees from Stanford University and is a professor of law emeritus at the University of Oklahoma, where he also served six years as associate dean for academics and associate director of the Law Center. He lives in the Ozark Hills of southern Missouri. He is the author or coauthor of fifteen books and more than a hundred magazine articles on military and western history.